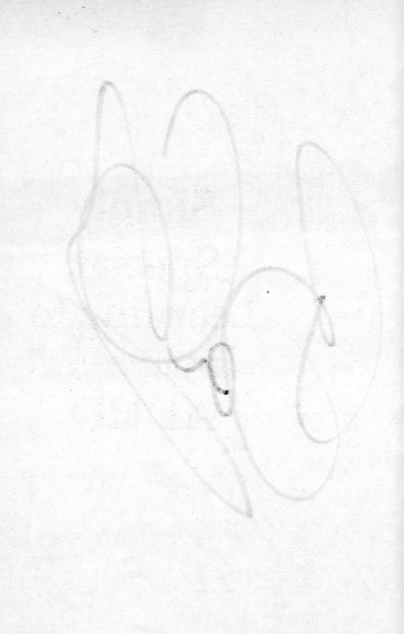

Simply Special:

First publishing 2007
Glenn, Ben
Simply Special; Learning to Love your ADHD
Ben Glenn p. cm.
Includes bibliographical references
ISBN 978-0-9675680-3-X (paperback)

1. *Attention Deficit hyperactivity in adolescence- Popular works.*

2. *Attention Deficit hyperactivity in adolescence- Life skills guides.*

3. *Attention Deficit hyperactivity in adults- Popular works.*

4. *Attention Deficit hyperactivity in adults- Life skills guides.*

I. *Glenn, Ben*   II. *Title*

Library of Congress Catalog Card Number: 2006935500

Other books by the Author
Big Enough: Finding Faith to Move Mountains

How to Contact the Author
Professional speaker Ben Glenn has been entertaining and educating audiences for more than a decade. He speaks about ADHD, having a positive attitude, achieving personal excellence and spiritual issues to groups all over the world. To discuss hiring him for your next conference, annual meeting, fund raiser or special event, contact:

Polina Osherov
Chalkguy Media International
www.chalkguy.com or 800-763-2609
email: polina@chalkguy.com

Dedication

*To my wife, Polina, for always seeing
the diamonds in the rough*

Acknowledgements

*Special thanks to my army of editors
(in no particular order):*

Polina Glenn
Christine Kirchman
Vladimir Osherov
Rebecca Woo
Jocelyn Godfrey
Larry Medcalfe
&
Melissa Glenn

Introduction

My Quest...
Your Quest

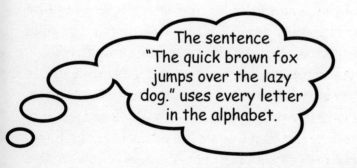

The sentence "The quick brown fox jumps over the lazy dog." uses every letter in the alphabet.

I was complaining the other day to someone about how long it has taken me to write this book, and how I really don't like to write, and that person asked me why I even bother writing if it's such a drag. Great question!

As strange as it may sound, one of the main reasons I write is because I am not very good at it. But, if I stop writing, I will never get better at it.

I had struggled so much with reading and writing in school that as a freshman in college, I spent my first semester in English 099. I was the only one in the class who was born on U.S. soil. It was a little embarrassing.

During second semester, in English 101, I met my future wife. She was fresh off the boat from Australia (though, as I was later to find out, she was actually Russian), and, because of the fact that I was a huge Nicole Kidman fan, she caught my ear with her cute Aussie accent. Our first class assignment was to write a page about what we did over our winter break and exchange it with a classmate to correct. I thought, what better way to meet this exotic beauty than to give her my paper? Maybe I can even ask her out on a date or something.

When all was said and done, I returned her paper unmarked, since I wasn't really able to read most of the big words she had used, and she gave me mine back along with three typed pages of corrections. At the very top of my paper she had written, "This is the worst piece of writing I have ever seen." And the rest, as they say, is history!

Another reason I write is because, unfortunately, my brain has a hard drive dating back to the early '90's. It's only got about 256 megabytes worth of space. Had I known I was going to run out of space so quickly, I would have asked for at least 20 gigabytes! As it is, I end up forgetting more than 80% of all the thoughts and ideas that ever pop into my mind and I hate it when I let a good idea get away. Writing stuff down in my "Magic Notebook" (which you will read about later on, and which helped inspire this book) helps me to stay organized and keep track of things I hear and see that I can later use in my programs or for my comedy.

Also, I write because I've decided that I hate being a quitter. Quitting is the easy, cowardly way out. It took me a while to realize this, but I finally made a decision that dyslexia or not, I was going to learn how to express my thoughts on paper. If I could get up on stage and speak, if I could pick up the phone and have a conversation, then surely I could sit down and type what was going through my mind.

Let me tell you, it's taken many years to get to a point where my first draft actually makes sense to people other than myself. Though I struggle to this day with grammar, spelling, tenses and punctuation, every time I sit down and start typing, I get a little bit better at it.

Dyslexia has been, and continues to be, a great struggle in my life, but it has not been my greatest. My biggest battle has been with ADD (Attention Deficit Disorder).

Side note: My editor tells me the disorder should be listed as ADHD and that ADDer should actually be listed as ADHDer, but ADD just rolls off the tongue easier and I think is easier to read, so just know that when I say ADD, I am talking about the disorder, and when I say ADDer, I am talking about someone who has it (rather than someone who really likes to add stuff up).

Back when I was first diagnosed with a learning disability (LD), not many people knew about ADD in the small school I attended, so it was overlooked. It wasn't until years later that I would receive the official label: ADD.

Since ADD has been the issue that I have struggled with the most, even before my official diagnosis, it has been ADD that I have worked the hardest to understand. Because of this, I wanted to let you know that most of what I will share throughout this book will be given from an ADDer's perspective. Don't let that discourage you from reading this book if you don't have ADD. Although a lot of the information in this book is ADD-specific, most of what I share applies to all individuals with learning disabilities or any other "label" that renders them "special."

Which leads to my last, but not least, reason for writing this book. I write because I know the information you'll find between these pages will help you. No matter where

I go and who I speak with about this subject, I find myself surrounded by adults and young people who either have some kind of a learning disability or ADD, or know someone who does. These folks have been telling me for years that they like the way I explain ADD. They say that my illustrations make a lot of sense and they wish that their brother, mother, son, sister or daughter had come with them to hear me speak. Fortunately, this book allows me the opportunity to let you "take me home with you" to share with whomever you think needs to hear my story and perspective on being labeled ADD.

In the movie *Indiana Jones and the Last Crusade*, Professor Henry Jones warns his son Indiana Jones of the final challenge that awaits them at the conclusion of their quest:

"He who finds the Grail must face the final challenge."

"What final challenge?" asks Indy looking a bit concerned.

"Three devices of such lethal cunning."

"Booby traps?"

"Oh yes. But I found the clues that will safely take us through, in the Chronicles of St. Anselm."

And it's with these clues that Indiana Jones dodges death once again, saves the day, and rides off into the sunset with the sounds of a great John Williams score playing in the background.

Lately, I have been thinking that learning to live with and manage ADD is like an exciting and difficult quest. I have found a definition of the word "quest" that I really like: "The journey a hero takes to achieve his goal." Another one that is not so glamorous sounding yet true: "A search for something, especially a long or difficult one." So you see, with any quest, there are going to be booby traps. I think it's some kind of a rule. It is my desire to tell you about some of these traps, and give you some secret weapons to use in combating them.

My hope for you as you read this book is that you will gain a glimpse into the heart and mind of someone else who learns and feels differently and has to live with being labeled. I am someone who has experienced some of the same obstacles you are now facing. I know how it feels to be alone, confused, and hopeless. I also know how to work with those feelings and find encouragement, relief, and joy. Finally, I have learned to see my learning challenges as a gift, rather than a handicap. This knowledge has led me to embrace my ADD and to be able to tell anyone who asks that I love being ADD!

If you are an ADDer, I believe that you will also be encouraged and inspired to see yourself from a whole different perspective. You deserve this encouragement.

If you are looking for freedom from the label and if you want to learn how ADD can be a blessing and not a curse, this book is for you.

I'm no one important, but I am an expert in this field. Why? Because I have first-hand knowledge of the subject. I've been there and done that and I hope that my experiences will be helpful to you. Whether you will agree with everything I share with you or not, believe this one thing: sometimes what appears to be an absolute tragedy in the moment, can, with time, become an utter blessing.

In the third grade, as I walked through the doors of the Special Ed classroom for the very first time, I thought I was getting a life "prison sentence." I couldn't have been more wrong.

1

I'm Special!

the Scoop

- Be sure to use the bathroom before going in for any kind of test
- A manila folder with your name and stamped 'X-File' is never a good thing

In the state of Illinois, in some stern government building, in the dark recesses of a damp basement, there are many filing cabinets, X-Files style, and in one of those is a file with my name on it. I'm sure of it. This file is about four inches thick and filled with papers that date all the way back to the year 1981. The file reads like a novel. "A long time ago in a land far, far away, there was a boy in the third grade who was asked to take some tests. They were long tests and took a lot of energy and concentration. Though he didn't know it, the tests they gave him were the beginning of an exciting journey - a journey on which our hero faced an uncertain future, stumbling many times, fighting for survival, and even teetering on the edge of self-destruction. A journey which is still in progress today..."

Back in 1981, I never could have imagined how some diagrams, charts and flash cards they used to test me would change my life. Nor could I have ever pictured that I would be where I am today. Everybody has several important turning points in their lives, days they look back at and say to themselves, "That's where it all started." Well, those tests and what followed were like that for me and I'd like to tell you a bit about it.

It all started with Mrs. Hill.

If you were to look up the definition of a "great teacher", you would find a picture of Mrs. Hill. The day I met Mrs. Hill, I knew it was going to be a great year. She stood at the door that first day, greeting each child who came into her classroom. She had short brown hair and eyes that twinkled when she smiled – which was often. She was the perfect height; not too tall, not too short and conveyed a sense of kindness and safety. She loved to wear long, flowery dresses and a sweet, flowery perfume to go along with them.

As we recited the Pledge of Allegiance that first day, I couldn't help but think as I watched my new enthusiastic, high energy teacher: "This lady is kinda cool." And she was! We were crazy about her. She was what a teacher was always meant to be, and she was one of my favorites.

Sometime, during the middle of the school year, Mrs. Hill noticed that I was not keeping up with the rest of the class. She began to give me extra help, even staying after school hours, in an effort to get me back up to speed. After a couple of months, despite her best efforts, there was little improvement. Though I spent hours doing extra work, I just wasn't "getting" the information that was being taught. Even as a third grader, I could tell that Mrs. Hill was quite frustrated. I don't think she was frustrated with me, but I think she was perturbed by the fact that she had a willing student, who appeared to be doing all the assigned and additional work, yet still could not grasp what was being taught. She finally decided that it was time to ask for help.

As a result, the school began testing me. The tests were given to me over the course of three days. Those weren't like any other tests I had ever taken. I sat at a round table in an otherwise empty classroom with an instructor who had several large, blue flip books. She would flip to one page in the book and ask me to count up the coins I saw there. Then she would flip to a totally different part of the book and ask me to find a pattern in some strange images. There was a whole lot of page flipping going on. At one point, I asked the instructor if she wanted me to help put the book back in order. I was afraid with all the flipping she had to do, she would get a paper cut.

Though I spent hours doing extra work, I just wasn't "getting" the information being taught.

I wondered why the school was having me tested. A small side of me hoped that I was suspected of being brilliant, and that the tests would allow me to skip grade school and move right into junior high. Maybe I was the next Doogie Howser?? (Teen genius who is a Doctor in a cheesy 80s TV Show.) And yet, I knew this couldn't be. I struggled with school, and as much as I feared the outcome of those tests, I knew deep down that they had been necessary.

At the end of all that testing, I was eager to get back to class. Since I was the only one being tested, I knew that the class would continue without me and I was afraid that I would be buried under a load of make-up homework. When I finally made it back to Mrs. Hill's classroom, I was relieved to be sitting at my own familiar desk. When class was done for the day, I walked up to Mrs. Hill's desk to see if she had make-up work for me to do in order to catch up with the rest of the class. She shook her head, smiling at me, rather sadly actually. She said, "Don't worry about all that, Ben. No make-up work for you to worry about."

I guess I must have looked at her like she was crazy because she quickly proceeded to tell me that my parents would be coming to meet with her in just a few minutes, and that I should sit and wait for them and not take the school bus home. The small alarm that went off inside my head when she told me not to worry about make-up homework turned into an air raid siren when she told me my parents were coming. This was NOT good! I knew that having both my parents called to the school for a parent-teacher meeting meant that something really bad was going to happen.

> **I was a good kid, but I was very easily distracted in class and that appeared to have an impact on my ability to learn.**

A little while later, as I sat at my desk inside the empty classroom contemplating the blackboard, both my parents appeared in the doorway. I will never forget the look on their faces. My mom looked worried; my dad, annoyed. I wanted to slide under the desk and disappear, but someone must have put super glue on my chair or something because I couldn't move. As I looked at my parents, I felt an unpleasant sensation rise up from the pit of my stomach, squeezing my heart and making it hard to breathe. I was really scared. What was going to happen to me now? As my parents approached me, glued as I was to the seat, I tried to forestall whatever punishment was coming. Since I didn't know what I had done wrong or why my parents had even been called to the meeting, I had no way of proving my innocence. I looked at them, and whispered "I didn't do anything."

Before we could speak, Mrs. Hill appeared with a manila folder under her arm. She asked me to wait while she and my parents met. I sat on the floor outside the classroom. I had expected the teacher to shut the door when she went inside to speak with my parents, but she did not. It was a minor oversight in the grand scheme of things, to be sure, but hearing what was exchanged in that room that afternoon was extremely demoralizing. Since I was only in the third grade, it was hard for me to understand everything that was being discussed, but one thing I couldn't fail to grasp was the fact that I was not brilliant. I heard Mrs. Hill talk about how poorly I had done on the tests, and with each word out of her mouth, any self-confidence I had began to leave me.

Mrs. Hill explained to my parents that I was different from the other students in the school because I didn't understand the information presented to me in class the way other children did. Meanwhile, what I heard her say was: "Your son is stupid."

She said that I was a good kid but I was very easily distracted in class and that appeared to have an impact on my ability to learn. My dad wondered if my problem was a matter of discipline and whether, with enough motivation, I would get back on track. But Mrs. Hill told my parents that it wasn't that I didn't try; it was as if there was "something else" keeping me from moving ahead. She then announced that based on the test results, I had officially been diagnosed as Learning Disabled. Oh joy! Not only was I stupid, but now I'd have to spend my life in a wheelchair too??!! This was too much. I felt tears starting to well up.

What was this curse "Learning Disability?" And of all the kids in the school, why did I have to become infected with it? It didn't help that on top of being absolutely terrified of losing the use of my legs, I heard a little voice inside telling me, "AND you're stupid." Indeed, a lot of people who receive the label "LD" believe just that: that they are stupid. (Which is completely and totally wrong, as I later realized.)

That evening, as my mother reassured me for what must have been the hundredth time that I would not be wheelchair bound, it was also becoming clear to me that getting this diagnosis meant all kinds of undesirable things. It meant that I would never be a "normal" kid again, or at least that is how I felt. I would forever be a loser. Dumb. Incompetent. Not brilliant in the least. It also meant that I would have to face all kinds of obstacles that other kids never even thought about.

Mrs. Hill gave my parents two options that day. The first option was to hold me back another year. Being held back a year was one of the most humiliating things I could think of. All my friends would be in the fourth grade while I was in the third...again! The idea of being left behind like that did not appeal to me at all.

Lucky for me, my dad would not hear of it.

"Next year you'll teach your class the same way you taught it this year," he said. "If he can't understand now because of a learning disability, what makes you think he will get this stuff next year? He'll still have the same learning disability. What we need to do is address the disability."

The second option was - effective immediately - to send me, full-time, to a special education class to see if what was left of the third grade could be salvaged. I wanted to yell, "Don't I have a say in the matter?" but no words would come out. It was as if someone punched me in the stomach and it knocked the wind out of me.

In my life, I have only been in two fist fights, aside from the occasional spat with my brothers. The first fight I got into was in the sixth grade. It was with a kid who used to be a really good friend of mine until he decided that it would be more fun to torment me instead of being my friend. One day we were pals and the next, he was calling me names and laughing at me. When the bus dropped us off by our house that day, we went at it for a good ten minutes. A group stood around cheering us on. When the fight was through, I was the one flat on my back with a bloody nose. I got my butt kicked big time! At least I got the chance to fight back. Sitting in that school hallway, it felt like I was getting my butt kicked and there was nothing I could do about it. The longer I sat there listening to the meeting, the more I felt defeated and helpless. I couldn't even raise a white flag and retreat. I had to sit there and take it!

The meeting finally concluded with my father making a decision. I was now officially a Special Ed student. I wasn't sure what that meant yet, but in my mind it was better than being held back a year, or so I thought.

Pep Talk Time

Getting "diagnosed" with anything is a huge bummer, isn't it? The word itself has a really scary, bad sound to it making you think of needles, pain and hospitals. Ugh! Thankfully, a diagnosis of ADD does not have to mean a death sentence. In fact, if you've been diagnosed and up to this point you have been terrified, angry, upset or totally confused by the whole thing, let me share some reassurance — you may not yet know it, but your diagnosis was really the beginning of what has every possibility of being a rather exciting adventure - a quest! I'm not saying it's going to be easy, mind you, so don't think that for a moment, what I am saying is that of all the things you could have been diagnosed with, ADD is one that you can actually use to make yourself and your life BETTER! I know you probably don't believe me right now, but keep reading and you might just change your mind.

Scratch-and-Sniff Stickers & a Horse Fly

the Scoop

- Trying to understand what's wrong with me
- Realizing that things will never be the same

31

An ostrich's eye
is bigger than
its brain.

Since the school I attended was small, it fell a little short in meeting the needs of Special Ed students. In fact, the year I became Special Ed was only the second year the school offered such a program.

I could swear that the Special Ed classroom had been a utility closet in its past life. It was that small. There was enough room for four desks, one of them the teacher's. The students' desks faced the only window in the room as if it was a large plasma screen TV. The only thing blocking the view of the outside world was a colorful collage of "well done" student assignments littered against the window as motivators, and also serving to shield the room from the hot, afternoon Midwest sun. The smell of artificial fruit and bubble gum hung in the air, cooked from the scratch-n-sniff stickers that peppered the assignments with praise. Those same stickers were slapped with words like "well done," "good job," and "excellent work."

From floor to ceiling and from one wall to the next were

shelves… shelves that perhaps at one point held Windex, buckets and mops, but now were cluttered with books, games, papers, crayons, markers, glue and candy.

The teacher's desk was much smaller than usual, as a larger desk would not have fit through the door. However, it displayed all the usual teaching equipment so you knew that the desk belonged to the boss and was not to be messed with. There was the typical Swingline stapler, a jar of thumb tacks, and paper clips. She had two baskets on the side of her desk; one was labeled "in" and the other "out" with a bright red marker. Both baskets were filled to the brim with assignments and other papers. The other side of her desk was inhabited by a large ceramic apple paperweight with a green worm sticking out the top. Hanging down the front of her desk was a collage of artwork crafted by past students declaring that she was the best teacher ever.

Finding my desk when I got to the classroom on the first day was easy. It was the only empty one there. I sat down and noticed how chipped it was, then raised my hand instantly. Even though I knew that I had a Learning Disability and needed the extra help, I still wasn't entirely clear on what it all meant. I needed answers.

> **Even though I knew that I had a Learning Disability and needed the extra help, I still wasn't clear on what it all meant.**

"Yes, Ben?" the teacher implored with a smile that looked artificially glued on, not the natural kind like Mrs. Hill wore.

"How long will I have to be here?," I asked, noticing a giant horsefly on one of the grape "well done" scratch-n-sniff stickers. (Did you know that there are around 3,000 different varieties of horse flies?)

The teacher looked a little taken aback. I guess she must have thought that I understood why I was there. She sighed when she saw what must have been a totally blank look on my face and did her best to explain what was going on. She repeated almost verbatim the words that I had heard Mrs. Hill share with my parents: all the tests I had taken showed that, while I was doing well in some areas of my schooling, in other areas I was well below average. For example, I had this thing called "dyslexia" which meant I saw letters and numbers backwards, and that was why I was having so much trouble in English class.

It kind of made sense, but then again it didn't. I strained hard to understand what she was telling me. It was difficult to concentrate because the horsefly had now waddled over to a drawing of a smiling clown and was smack dab in the middle of his red nose, looking like a large mole or worse a booger.

What finally got my full attention was when she said that I would need to come to the Special Ed classroom for the rest of the year, and that, more than likely, I would have to spend the next several years in such a class.

The fly forgotten, one realization overwhelmed me: I would never again be taught by Mrs. Hill. I would never again be in the same class as my friends.

I didn't know what to say. I wanted to disagree. I wanted to convince her that there had been a terrible mistake; that there was another boy by the name of Ben

Glenn who was supposed to be sitting where I was, but the words stuck in my throat.

I felt my head spinning a bit with the understanding that I was to be excluded from the life I had lived, placed with strangers, in a classroom I could barely fit in, a classroom that smelled like fruit and Windex and felt like a prison.

"Oh, okay," I finally mustered. But I was not okay. The universe I had lived in had just been turned inside out and I felt completely lost. It was as though I had landed on another planet, one that resembled my home planet yet somehow nothing about it felt right. I wanted my old life back, but I knew now that I could never get it back.

Years later, when I watched *The Shawshank Redemption* for the first time, I found myself relating, in retrospect, to Andy Dufresne; I was a prisoner with a life sentence for a crime I did not commit.

Pep Talk Time

Sometimes, change is not a good thing, but mostly we just don't like it because it makes us uncomfortable. Do you prefer to bury your head in the sand and pretend like nothing is wrong? Are you more afraid of the unknowns that come with change than the pain of living with a really ugly situation?
Is it time for a change in your life?
Have you been diagnosed with ADD, but are acting like nothing's happened? It's scary to have to change your routine and the way you do things, but in this case, you'll only be harming yourself if you continue acting as if your life is the same it was before your diagnosis. If you are struggling in school, if you can't keep up with your work, if you're hiding bad grades from friends and family, you need to ask yourself some serious questions. It might be time to step out and step up. The only way you'll be able to live an honest life and not sneak around hiding your struggles is if you come clean and get someone to help you. Believe me! There is no shame in that. It takes guts!

"I can suck pudding up my nose and blow
it out the corner of my eye, but they *still*
won't put me in the gifted class at school!"

3

Jumping, Leaping and Hopping to conclusions

the Scoop

- Jumping to the wrong conclusion can hurt you
- You are not alone
- Celebrate all things ADD
- Educate yourself about ADD

The first toilet seat ever seen on television was on "Leave it to Beaver."

Even after multiple explanations, it was REALLY hard for me to fully grasp what was happening to me and how going to a "special" classroom would help. I didn't feel that much different from my usual self. So I wasn't that good at reading and writing. So what? Did I really have to be punished in this way? I wasn't loud and obnoxious like Bobby and I wasn't a bully like Phil. I was a good kid. I did my best to do what Mrs. Hill asked of me. It was all so unfair and confusing.

I did my best to ignore the reality of my situation. I wasn't that successful, though, because inside of me a tape recorder on a permanent loop was replaying phrases and words like "slow learner", "dyslexia", "special needs", "needs extra help" and "learning disability". I was still having trouble connecting all the dots, but because I had already asked for an explanation more than once and because I didn't want to contribute more evidence to the idea that I was in fact, stupid, a part of me felt like I could not ask for any more clarification. I started coming to my own conclusions, which was a really, really bad idea. I ended up creating a picture in my head that was actually worse than, and far from, reality. It might have really helped to know the facts! Alas, I was young and scared and very self-conscious. It's no great surprise then that very soon, my reality was looking gloomy indeed.

◇◇◇◇◇◇◇◇◇◇◇◇◇◇◇◇◇◇◇◇◇◇◇◇◇

In the movie *Daredevil*, Elektra Natchios plays hard-to-get with Matt Murdock, a blind attorney who simply wants to know her name. By far the best scene in the movie is on a playground where we see Elektra and Matt sparring back and forth while continuing to discuss the disclosure of Elektra's name. "Do you do this to every guy who asks for your name?" Asks Matt as Elektra aims a roundhouse at his head.

There are anywhere between 15 and 18 million ADDers walking the earth

"You should try asking for my number," Elektra teases as she misses Matt's head by an inch.

Of course the two characters hit it off and become friends. As the movie progresses, we learn that Matt is actually Daredevil, a super hero, whose sole purpose is to fight crime. In the movie, while Daredevil is pursuing a villain named Bullseye, Elektra's father is killed. Everyone watching the movie knows that Elektra's father is killed by Bullseye, but Elektra assumes that it is Daredevil who is responsible for her father's death. Unaware that Daredevil is actually Matt and not knowing all the facts, she vows revenge.

Elektra does what so many of us tend to do: She jumps to a conclusion without having the full story. Then she gets mad and refuses to listen to reason.

Did you know that at one point people believed that the world was flat? It's true. I bet that a long time ago some person who was probably famous woke up and decided that during his next public appearance he would proclaim that the world was flat, and since all famous people know everything about everything (don't they?), everyone believed that the world was flat.

Whether or not the rumor of a flat world spread this way or not, the fact still remains that it wasn't until someone actually took a journey of discovery that we learned that the world is indeed round.

This has happened to me more times than I would like to admit. I jump to a conclusion or form an opinion based on incomplete information. I think it happened to me even last week. I called up a friend and he sounded weird and acted like he didn't want to talk to me. Our conversation ended quickly and I was left to wonder what I had done to make him mad. My imagination went wild. I spent the better part of a day putting together a mental list of all the possible things I could have done to offend him.

Two days later, I found out the full story. When I had called him, my friend was at the doctor's office about to get a procedure done that was painful and unpleasant. His tone and manner had nothing to do with me, but everything to do with being at the doctor's office. And to think that I wasted all that time obsessing about what I'd done to make him mad! All I had to do was ask!

I should know better now, but back in the third grade, I really had no idea. Sometimes I wonder how different things might have been if I knew then what I know now about being "special". Believe me when I tell you how blessed you are to be living during the "information age". Not to mention that these days they have a much better understanding of how the brain works. But back then, learning disorders weren't nearly as well understood or brought up in conversations.

In my imaginary world, my future was doomed...

So the way things were back in 1981 made it easier for me to just slink into a corner and come up with my own answers. I really hope that you don't make the same silly mistake and I have to believe that if you are reading this book, you are ready and willing to do what it takes to take life by the horns!

So anyway, in third grade, I knew I had a learning disability, but that was about the only fact in my possession. In my imaginary world, my future was doomed, I would be stuck in my closet of a classroom until my dying day and for all I knew, my legs would fall off tomorrow. I was also stupid and no one would like me. I'd never have any friends or play any sports. There really wasn't anything to look forward to. Mine was a sad life to say the least.

Moreover, I had not yet been diagnosed with ADD, and had I actually taken the time to understand LD and its implications, there still would have been a lot of unexplainable stuff going on with me that could only be explained by having ADD. Man, what a mess!

And it got worse! On top of feeling stupid and worthless, I then fell into the booby trap of believing I was the only one in the world who had such struggles. After all, I didn't know anyone else going through this.

Probably the worst thing about my situation was that I didn't know how to stop myself from jumping to all the wrong conclusions. I wish someone would have told me the following:

1. You are not alone. Read that one more time, to let it sink in - **you are not alone**. There are anywhere between 15 and 18 million ADDers walking the earth, and many millions more with other special learning disabilities. We are taking over, Baby! Think about that for a moment - there are millions of us out there struggling with a lot of the same stuff and millions of us coming up with ideas and solutions to help us make the most of our lives. You have every opportunity to be a success! There is hope!

2. EDUCATE YOURSELF! I can't even begin to tell you about the number of resources currently available to tell you about ADD and other Learning Disorders. Remember the end of *Raiders of the Lost Ark* when the Ark is packed into a large wooden crate and wheeled through a gigantic warehouse to be safely stored? That warehouse and all the thousands of crates it contains may be about how much information is available today about ADD. If reading is hard for you, ask your friends, parents, and teachers to read the info and tell you about it or read the information together and talk about what you read.

3. Get with the other ADDers and encourage one another. Enjoy being around other people who know how

you feel and struggle with the same issues. Brainstorm ways to make life easier. Share information and resources. Don't be afraid to say, "Hey! I've got ADD too!"

4. Always remember somewhere in the back of your overly-active, easily-distracted mind that you are not alone. (Did I already say that?)

Pep Talk Time

ADDers are the most outgoing people in the world. Many of you can be described as extroverts, which means that you're a very outgoing person who likes to be in the thick of things. That's great! So why not use your outgoing personality to ask for help? You were not built to take a back seat. You know you have struggles and though it's more comfortable to try and ignore them, you also know they could get worse. So ask for help. Sure, it may be a little scary… but it is a whole lot less scary than trying to figure things out on your own. Talk to your parents and be honest with them about your struggles. They will respect your honesty and find encouragement from your motivation. If your parents are not supportive, speak with a teacher, a guidance counselor or another sympathetic adult like a coach or a youth pastor. Remember the saying, "Together we stand; divided we fall." Find the other ADDers around you and encourage one another. Learn from one another and, by all means, be ADD with one another! A group of normal people in a room together is called a gathering. A group of ADDers in a room together is called a party! You are not alone!

The Ritalin Controversy

the Scoop

- The use of ADD drugs is highly controversial
- Don't just take someone else's word for it - do your own research to find out if ADD drugs are right for you
- Peanut Butter Bars are the Cadillac of Little Debbie Cakes

NEW SAFETY UNDERWEAR WITH
WEDGIE-SENSITIVE AIRBAGS

Early in my adult years I came to two conclusions: I struggle because of ADD and all ADD medication is evil. I was accurate with the first, but naively off target with the second. I rode this erroneous bandwagon for quite a while after hearing a talking head spout off how awful ADD drugs were. The talking head said that a lot of kids were being over-medicated. I didn't know any better, so I figured that sounded about right. The talking head said that kids today just didn't know the meaning of the word "respect" and because there is some truth to that, I nodded my head and bought the whole argument.

Fact was, though, that I didn't know a thing about ADD medication. I was just taking for granted that whoever made those comments knew what they were talking about. Being an ADDer myself, before I got a better understanding of how ADD medication worked, I thought that ADDers really didn't need to take anything. Plus, deep down inside, I had always wondered if maybe

I had been born with the "lazy/crazy" gene and maybe that was my problem. Because I had made it thus far without medication, why couldn't other ADDers make it? So without further analysis, I made up my mind that ADD drugs were bad. Imagine my surprise and frustration when I found out that I had allowed myself to be misled. Here's what happened:

Years on the road and traveling from one event to another had taken their toll on my health. I was carrying an extra 60 pounds, felt tired most of the day and ate the least nutritious food I could find. I was a frequent flier at fast food restaurants and Little Debbie and I were the bestest of friends. My pants were tight, and XXXXL shirts were in my near future at the rate I was going. I was becoming the Chunky Chalkguy! Finally, one day I just couldn't take it anymore. I signed up with a Personal Trainer, got a Little Debbie Patch and cut back on the junk food. My trainer suggested I try an

I was becoming the Chunky Chalkguy!

Ephedra supplement to curb my appetite and speed up my metabolism. (This was before the Ephedra ban when this supplement was still seen as effective and relatively safe.) After a few weeks of religiously taking Ephedra, I saw some amazing results. Not only was I losing weight and feeling physically better than I had in years, but it was as if my mind had also undergone a transformation. I was motivated, focused, directed. I was reading, writing, getting projects completed. Amazing! Occasionally, my wife would look at me suspiciously and say, "Who are you and what have you done with my husband?" Honestly, we were both surprised and excited by the changes that were taking place in my life. I had become a new man. We speculated about what had suddenly made such a difference in my attitude and ability to stay focused and motivated, but could never quite put a finger on it. Eventually, we stopped trying to solve the mystery and just assumed that I had turned over a new leaf because it had just been the right time for it.

Instead of being a Superhero, I was back to my old unmotivated, distracted self...

Then one day, it was time to re-stock on my supplement and I noticed that the packaging had changed somewhat and now said "Ephedra-free" on it. I didn't think much of it.

A week later though, something just wasn't right with me. I was tired more. I had been getting up at 6:30 in the morning consistently to read and write, but suddenly, I just didn't feel like it any more. I would sit in my office and instead of attacking a project with energy, I would procrastinate and shuffle papers. What was going on? Instead of being a Superhero, I was back to being my old, unmotivated, distracted self. I don't know if you can imagine how frustrating and confusing that was. Picture having some super power like being able to leap tall buildings or catching bullets in your hand and then suddenly being stripped of these talents. Not fun, right?

I tried very hard to regain some of the motivation and drive that I had experienced in the months before, but it was like climbing a very steep mountain. I just couldn't keep up the pace.

Fortunately, during my months of productivity and with encouragement from my wife, I started to take a tele-class through OFI (Optimal Functioning Institute) about ADD and becoming an ADD coach. (Eventually, I decided that coaching wasn't for me, but everything I learned during those classes I have been able to put to use in my presentations and writing.). One day, as I was struggling to stay focused on a tele-lecture about ADD medication, something the instructor said caught my attention. It was time for one of those "duh!" moments. Turns out that Ephedra, a stimulant (just like Ritalin), had been unofficially used by some people to treat their ADD symptoms. Mind you this was not anything that the medical community endorsed, but somehow, some folks had figured out that taking Ephedra was helping their ADD symptoms. Suddenly, everything clicked into place. Now, I understood what had been happening to me all those months. Without knowing it, I had been taking a "medication"!

There are anywhere between 15 and 18 millions ADDers walking the earth

It was at this point that I realized that maybe the talking heads spouting off about ADD medication didn't really have all the answers. It became clear to me that even though I had managed all those years to get through life and school without resorting to meds, I had also missed out on a level of productivity and achievement that was far above average. I was actually kind of mad about it, like I'd been cheated or something. Still, I was the one who didn't do my homework and when I was honest with myself, I knew that I had no one to blame but myself.

Not long after this, I set up an appointment with my family doctor and told her that I was interested in trying out an ADD medication so I could get back to my early morning reading and writing sessions. I hadn't even realized that there were so many other ADD drugs apart from Ritalin (Guess I wasn't paying attention in the tele-class!). Turned out there were all kinds of ADD medications available because not every ADDer was the same. So I tried out Concerta, then Strattera, then Adderal, and finally ended up using Ritalin because it worked the best for me. I'm one of those people who responds well to stimulants.

Before using stimulants (at first, unknowingly, Ephedra and then with full knowledge, Ritalin), there were things I just couldn't do. Sure, I survived school, but I made it by compensating and finding ways to avoid the tasks I struggled with the most. For example, I never enjoyed reading. It was too hard to stay focused and remember what I'd just read.

Now most mornings, I read. Sometimes, it's a devotional, sometimes, a chapter in a book, sometimes it's a long email from someone who saw me at a program and has questions. And now I'm reading because I actually enjoy it. How crazy is that? I read stuff I don't have to read AND I enjoy it! There is no doubt in my mind that my medication has a significant effect on my brain chemistry.

Can I function without taking Ritalin? Sure! Do I become a key-losing, appointment-forgetting, conversation-disrupting scatter brain without it? Well, no, not quite. But, with it do I operate and think on a completely different and more satisfying level? Absolutely! I think that ADD medication is much like prescription glasses: You can see a little without them, but with them, everything is clear. I am living proof that an ADDer can be made more functional with the help of a prescription much like insulin makes a diabetic more functional. Telling an ADDer that they shouldn't at least try out an ADD medication is like telling your friend who wears Coke-bottle-thick glasses, "Sure, go ahead and take my car for a drive without your glasses. You really don't need them." It's a wreck waiting to happen.

There are many medication available to treat some of the symptoms of ADD

Am I saying that everyone who has ADD absolutely needs or should be taking one medication or another? No! What I'm saying is that getting help with your symptoms in the shape of a pill is an option that you should definitely consider, especially if you have already tried other methods of helping you manage your particular challenges. Talk with your parents and family doctor. If they can't help answer your questions, talk to a specialist. Talk to other ADDers. Don't be afraid to ask questions. I know that being on meds in school is a stigma, but wouldn't you rather be able to get your work done and get the teachers off your back than to try and pretend that you don't dread coming to school every day?

If you are one of the many who already takes medication, still do your homework. Learn all about your particular prescription – how it works, possible side effects and dosing. How are you to know what it should or shouldn't do unless you ask questions? Become more proactive in managing your ADD and not just when it comes to medication.

I can't stress this enough: education is the key! I know that "education" is a word that we ADDers don't necessarily like a whole lot, but there's no getting around it if you want to take control of your ADD and make it work for you. Jim Rohn (a leading motivational speaker and entrepreneur) says it best: "What you don't know will always hurt you." The fact that I didn't know anything about ADD when I was a student hurt me. The fact that I was misinformed about ADD medication hurt me. Lack of knowledge was a greater problem than ADD itself!

A word of caution: As an ADDer, even in college, I was never big into reading and "research", so I had a tendency to look for easy answers. Cliffs Notes was a lifestyle for me! On some subjects, I often got suckered into taking the word of a talk show host or a celebrity, and letting his or her opinion become mine as if it were fact but in doing so, I did myself a great disservice.

So... Read the books, watch the programs, listen to the tapes, go online and network with other people with ADD, but take your time forming an opinion. Make sure that what you believe is based on more than one source of information, especially if that source is mainstream media. I don't know about you, but I've noticed that the media usually likes to highlight stories that are either dramatic or sensational in some way - so the information being shared with the average consumer is often selectively presented, meaning you don't get the full picture. Convenient for ratings, just not great if you're trying to make the best possible decision to get your life on track.

While writing this book, I did a lot of research and reading to make sure that what I put in this book was as accurate as possible. I was amazed by the number of different theories, treatment options, and controversies that are out there about ADD. There are a lot of myths as well. My two favorites are: 1) ADD does not really exist – all these kids need is some old-fashioned discipline in their lives and 2) ADD does not really exist - the pharmaceutical industry invented the disease so that they could make billions in Ritalin sales. And of course everything I read is in its own way very convincing. It really can be hard to separate fact from fiction, but that shouldn't stop you from trying.

If you're going to have an opinion about ADD and what it means to you, don't base that opinion on only half of the information. Make sure that whatever you think about this whole subject is based on information coming from a variety of sources. And don't be afraid to ask questions!

◇◇◇◇◇◇◇◇◇◇◇◇◇◇◇◇◇◇◇◇◇◇◇◇

When I was in high school, I asked my doctor how I got LD and Dyslexia. He shrugged and told me that there were so many possible factors involved that one could never know for sure. That wasn't exactly helpful, but because he was a doctor and I was just a "special" teenager, I didn't question him further. It wasn't until years later that I decided that I shouldn't just sit back and allow myself to walk around with a diagnosis and a label that made no sense to me. (I hope you don't wait as long as I did!)

I decided not to allow my symptoms to run my life, but rather to learn how I could make them work for me. If you consider taking the same approach when it comes to your particular challenges, I believe that there is a very real possibility that you too will claim to "love" your ADD at some point in your life.

Pep Talk Time

Don't let anyone tell you what ADD should mean in your life. Figure it out for yourself. Don't be afraid to ask questions. You have every right to ask your doctor what this pill or that pill is for. And if they use a big word that doesn't make sense, then you need to become like a broken record and ask "What does that mean?"

"What does that mean?"

"What does that mean?"

"What does that mean?"

"What does that mean?"

Remember, education is key. I know that "E" word sends chills up your spine, but remember that you are a creative individual. Creativity is one of the awesome qualities that comes packaged with ADD, so use it to take advantage of all the resources available to you. I know some of these resources are packaged in a way that doesn't play to your strengths, but with your creative mind you can find a way to make them work for you. Do not allow ADD to happen to you, but take charge and make ADD work in your life.

5 The Fellowship Chip

the Scoop

- Sasquatches need hugs too
- Love, acceptance and support feed our souls
- When you "make the fridge" you know that you done good!
- ADDers love to play - make it (whatever 'it' is) fun!

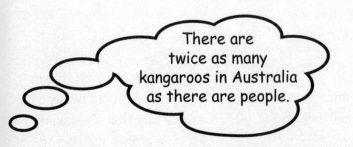

There are twice as many kangaroos in Australia as there are people.

As I sat in that storage closet of a classroom back in the third grade, I looked around and was astounded at what a difference a week had made in my life. I left behind a classroom that held 30 students, half of whom I called friends, to be in a classroom of three students, myself included. For the first time in my life I got a full dose of feeling alone.

I don't recall my new classmates' names, but for the sake of my story, I'll call them Betty and Bob. Betty had Down's Syndrome. She was also one of the nicest people I had ever met. In fact, she had such a great smile that when I saw her for the first time, I almost forgot I was in a bad mood. That year, Betty was one of the people who made it a little easier to go to that Special Ed classroom. Betty loved to play the games that lined the shelves all around the room, and since I'm a big gamer, we hit it off right away. The most unique thing I remember about Betty was the fact that she loved giving hugs! It didn't matter if you were only just being introduced to her, you were getting a hug. I admit I was a little taken aback initially, but as the days went on, I began to look forward to them. I was going through one of the hardest times in my life, and as much as I wanted to be the tough kid, a hug now and then felt great.

> **...one can of Jolt has as much caffeine as six cans of Mountain Dew...**

Bob was a good kid who just drank too much Jolt. (Jolt is a classic soda that came out in the '80's. It's been said that one can of Jolt had as much caffeine as six cans of Mountain Dew). Bob had been diagnosed with something called BD, a Behavioral Disorder. Thankfully, Bob wasn't a bully, and after one day in the room with Bob, I wanted to take him home. Trust me, that kid was pure entertainment. Watching him was like watching a television show with lots of explosions in fast-forward. I'm not sure if it's legal anymore, but the only way our teacher could keep Bob in his seat was by using duct tape. (You might not want to suggest this to your teachers today. I'm sure they would get into trouble. Scotch tape, on the other hand, might be acceptable... Just kidding!).

All in all, my new classmates were okay, and I was thankful for the fact that I wasn't in that classroom all by myself. But I still felt isolated from the rest of the world.

Back then and on through high school, if someone were to ask me, "What's the most important thing in your life right now?" besides family, I was sure to answer 'friends.'

In fact, I would say that academics were at the very bottom of my priority list, unless they had some potential influence on gaining friends. It was unimaginable to not have friends. I could not think of a worse punishment.

Why is friendship so important to all of us? I like to think that we were created with a "fellowship chip." We're sociable creatures designed for having relationships. It is completely normal to want to be accepted by those around us. Without family and friends, our lives would be pretty shallow.

After all, we depend on each other for our survival. No, most of us don't go out and hunt with each other anymore for our dinner, but we depend on our mailman, our grocer, the guy who fixes our mom's car, all of whom provide services that make our lives complete. We wouldn't want to upset our barber, baby sitter, neighbor... because they give something to us.

On a more subtle level, we depend on our family and "friends," our peers, to provide acceptance, a hug, advice... the things we might call "love," in its various forms. This is also a normal part of life. Love, acceptance, and support can feed our soul.

Unfortunately, many relationships can bring us about as much pain as pleasure. In an ideal world everyone would get along. Kids wouldn't pick on one another, parents wouldn't go through bitter divorces, rival gang members wouldn't shoot each other down in the streets and terrorism would not be a word anyone would know the meaning of. But the reality is much different. Somewhere in the history of man, an unspoken standard was formed. If you're different, if you don't look, speak, dress, worship, believe a certain, specific way, then you are considered a weirdo at best and an enemy to be hunted down and killed at worst.

The movie, *Forrest Gump*, has a great scene where the

"unspoken standard" I'm talking about is shown in a simple and heart-breaking way. It's the first day of school, and Forrest gets on the school bus for the first time ever. He walks up those three steps, and turns to see every kid on the bus staring at him. Without even exchanging a greeting with this young kid with leg braces, but based on physical appearance alone, most students on the bus decide that he is not worthy of their friendship. They waste no time letting him know that he's a misfit. As he makes his way down the bus looking for an empty seat, these kids make it no secret that they don't want him sitting next to them.

The beauty of this movie for me, though, is the fact that in spite of being "special," Forrest goes on to live a life filled with adventure, success and love.

I was a student once and I know that all young people battle daily with trying to fit in. Yes, even the "normal" kids have their moments of insecurity. The idea of being left out, left behind, picked last, and forgotten, certainly haunted me and filled me with much grief and frustration. It also prompted me to make some unfortunate and cringe-inducing fashion choices like wearing parachute pants with a tucked in t-shirt and pastel polos with white pants and loafers with no socks. (Please don't think badly of me!! I didn't know what I was doing!)

Naturally, getting diagnosed with anything only makes the problem of fitting in multiply by 1,000.

As you can imagine, the first few weeks in the Special Ed classroom weren't easy. My teacher probably wondered if they made a mistake by putting me in her class instead of holding me back a year.

More than anything I was confused and afraid. I wasn't

sure what I was supposed to be doing. I still felt like the old me, but suddenly the people I had contact with were treating me differently and I didn't much like it. I wanted things to go back to the way they were, but of course the situation was completely outside my control. I had no idea what to do so I shut down. Even though there were only three students in the class, and I had every opportunity to ask questions and request help, I didn't. I sat at my desk with a long face, counting holes in the ceiling tile or trying to figure out how they got the scratch-n-sniff stickers to smell like fruit. I was actually counting down the weeks to summer. For some reason, I let my imagination convince me that if I made it to summer, come fourth grade, everything would return to normal. It had to!

The idea of being left out, left behind, picked last, and forgotten, certainly haunted me and filled me with much grief and frustration.

Meantime, my poor Special Ed teacher was losing patience with me. One day, when I refused to complete a simple writing exercise, she lost it.

"Ben, SNAP OUT OF IT!" She looked like she wanted to shake me.

"If you sit here and do nothing, you will end up with nothing. Let me help you. I can show you the way, but you have to get involved. I know you have what it takes, and I know that with some hard work, you can get better at reading and writing. You can't give up! I know this has all just fallen in your lap, but you do have a choice to make: Quit or push through. I think you have too much to offer to surrender, so I hope you choose to fight back.

Let's do this thing together."

Trust me, it was quite a pep talk. My grandmotherly looking, mild-mannered teacher could give William Wallace in *Braveheart* a run for his money when it came to motivating the troops! With my wild ADDer imagination, I can easily picture her closing out her little speech by leaping to her feet and screaming "FREEDOM" at the top of her lungs. She did no such thing, of course, but the message was loud and clear all the same. Her passion actually inspired me to ask her to explain what was wrong with me.

She repeated what I had already known, that I had a learning disability, but I wanted more information,

The taste of victory was unforgettable. I wanted to feel this way more often!

"Does that mean I'm stupid?"

"Of course not!" She exclaimed. "We all have our struggles, but we all also have something to offer."

"Then what does it mean?" I said more confused than ever.

She looked as if she were going to take on the English army herself and said, "All I know is that you learn things differently from other kids and that's YOUR struggle. We might not figure out exactly why that is, but we can definitely try and figure out how to help you with this struggle. And also we can work together find the things that you ARE good at." She gave me a kindly smile. " Ben, I know that you don't like the way things have turned out this year. I know you might feel scared and alone. One thing I can tell you is that you are not alone. We can work together to make things better. Would you like that?

I guess I must have nodded 'yes'. Something about her conviction must have rubbed off on me because in that moment I was neither afraid nor feeling like I was all alone. I liked the idea that maybe there was something that I was really good at. I spent the rest of that year actually trying to learn and improve my reading and writing skills. I also had another reason to work hard. Before my teacher was done with her pep talk, she also made me a deal. She said, "If you work hard for the rest of the year and show improvement, I will recommend that next year the school lets you have at least one class period in a mainstream level class."

My efforts were rewarded with a few small victories, like the first time I wrote my name, and it looked like my name. Up until that point, I had really sloppy handwriting (that's what you do when you can't spell). You scribble a few loops and lines so that it might kind of look like the word you're trying to spell, but no one can really tell what it is. They just have to take your word for it.

So the day I learned how to spell my name was a good day. It wasn't easy. It took me many tries. I remember getting frustrated and wanting to quit after failing a dozen times to keep the letters orderly and legible. But the moment I carefully and painstakingly with tongue-sticking-out finally wrote out B E N, and it actually looked like it, my Special Ed teacher was right there, congratulating me on a job well done.

The taste of victory was unforgettable. I wanted to feel this way more often. During recess, which was with all the "normal" kids, I went up to students I didn't even know, held out my paper, pointed at my name, and said with great pride, "Yep, it's my name! I wrote it!!"

◇◇◇◇◇◇◇◇◇◇◇◇◇◇◇◇◇◇◇◇◇◇◇◇◇◇◇◇

I reaped the benefits of being in such a small class because my teacher paid close attention to the way my mind worked, and she experimented with different methods to help me learn and stay focused. One of the first things she did was pull my desk away from the window. She faced my desk toward hers so she could read my expressions and notice when it appeared that my brain was going adrift. She took my assignments and combined them with fun interactive games in order to keep my mind engaged. Now you all know that we ADDers love to play. If you can make work fun, stimulating, adventurous, and less boring, we will be with you every step of the way. She broke down complex ideas that my mind couldn't grasp into smaller, manageable pieces. She continued to change things up to keep me on my toes. She learned that what worked one day didn't always work the next.

The one thing I'll never forget was the constant repetition. I can still hear her voice sometimes reminding me of some task she was trying to pound into my head. We ADDers tend to have a difficult time with memorization "on the fly". So my teacher was like a broken record: She would repeat everything to me at least five to ten times a day. On top of that, she would always have me repeat back to her what she just reminded me to do, just to make sure I couldn't pull out the old, "I didn't hear you; I'm special" excuse.

Any time my mind would begin to drift, my teacher was there, reminding me what my task was. Every day I walked into that classroom, our purpose was spelled out so no one would be confused as to why we were there.

In the best selling book, <u>Purpose Driven Life</u>, the author, Rick Warren, explains the importance of organizations and people in general having a **purpose statement** in order to reach their goals. Warren believes that to be an effective tool, a purpose statement should be reviewed every 30 days. For ADDers, I believe that a purpose statement needs to be reviewed every 30 minutes! At least I am sure that's what it felt like to my Special Ed teacher, because she was relentless, especially once she figured out that repetition really worked for me.

> **You know when you "make the fridge", you done good!**

All that hard work eventually paid off. I remember one test in particular. It was in my worst subject; English. I studied so hard for that test that when it was time to take it, I was actually excited. You might be thinking that I must be "special" if I got excited to take a test, but what you have to understand is that I had never studied that hard before in my life and for the first time I was actually confident that I would do well.

I completed the test in record time and turned it in. The worst part was waiting all weekend to find out how I scored. You know what I was doing all weekend, don't you? Doubting myself and putting myself down. By Monday I had managed to convince myself that I had done so poorly on the exam that they would keep me in Special Ed for the rest of my life. When my teacher placed the corrected test paper on my desk, I covered my eyes. I was too afraid to see the results. I hated being a failure. I was tired of doing poorly, and a poor grade on this test would have been devastating because I had worked so hard to prepare for it. I wouldn't look at the score as long as I could stand it, but soon my curiosity got the better of me and I slowly peeled my hands away from my face, finger by finger, looked down, and there it was, a big C-...!

IT WAS THE BEST GRADE I HAD EVER GOTTEN!

I jumped out from behind my desk, ran over to Bob, and started to hand out high fives. I might have even done a couple of victory laps around the classroom, if the teacher hadn't pulled out a huge roll of duct tape from behind her desk and asked me if I was feeling lucky that day. I jumped back in my seat! I was so excited, I couldn't keep still in my seat and my face had a huge, crazy grin on it. And then, just when I thought things couldn't get any better, I noticed it. There, right by the grade, was the ultimate prize, a grape-scented scratch-n-sniff sticker! It was round and purple and had a picture of grapes on it. I rubbed, scratched, sniffed, and clawed that thing all day. For the first time since my diagnosis, I felt like a winner, instead of a loser.

When I got home from school, I galloped up to my mom with the paper in hand like I'd won the lottery. She took one look at my grade and was never more proud. Do you know what she did with that paper? Oh, you know what she did! She put that bad boy on the fridge, and you know when you "make the fridge", you done good! I was on my way!!

At the end of the school year, our little LD group had a party... lots of pizza, candy, and pop, which was very entertaining, especially when Bob gulped down about four cans of the fizzy stuff. You might have had first-hand experience with what a six-pack of caffeinated pop can do for a normal child, now multiply that by ten, and that was what we had going on at the party.

Before I left to go home that day, my Special Ed teacher took me aside and said,

"You did it. You kept up your end of the bargain and improved more in the last couple of months than I ever expected. So, I am going to keep my promise to you. I am going to recommend that the school allows you an hour a day in a mainstream level class. "

"YES!"

Pep Talk Time

Sometimes the hardest thing about an unexpected transition or an unwelcome change in our lives is that we feel like we're alone and that can be a scary thing. How you respond to the change is probably the most important factor in whether the change will be a good or a bad thing in your life. Shut down and you'll not only miss out on the possibilities, but also stop growing as a person. My teacher was right; we do all have our struggles, but we also have something to offer. Sometimes, our gifts and talents are to be found in the midst of our struggles. Don't be discouraged if it seems like nothing is going right - you are more than the sum of your challenges. Remember, negativity is always easier than keeping up a positive outlook, but it is also incredibly destructive. Moping, cursing life, others, God and having a sour face on day in and day out will always hurt you first and foremost. So take heart and celebrate even the smallest of victories!

Cartoon copyrighted by Mark Parisi, printed with permission

6 Cheating 101

the Scoop

- Making cheat sheets can help anyone pass a test
- If you ever play Monopoly with my brother Chris, watch out! He cheats!
- Remember to spell-check all your love notes

You burn
more calories
sleeping that you
do watching TV.

When the fourth grade rolled around, I was pumped. I was proud of what I had accomplished in the Special Ed classroom, but having friends and feeling "normal" was more important to me now than ever. I was excited to be heading back down to the right wing of the school.

As soon as the bus dropped us off, I felt pride swell my chest. I walked into that school with my head held high, wearing my new Wranglers and a yellow-navy-green, striped polo shirt. I felt a steady confidence that *this* was going to be a great year for me. When I came to the part of the school hallway where I had gotten used to turning left for Special Ed classes, I felt a chill run up my spine. Today, I turned to the right. I walked down that hallway with all the "normal" kids and it felt great to be back in the middle of things.

When I found my classroom, I was thrilled to see that stuck to the front of one of the thirty lidded desks was a piece of bright blue, card stock paper with my name. Ben

Glenn: That's me!

I loved the desks with lids. I always had fun putting my pencil at the top of the desk and watching it roll down. Sometimes I would race a pen against a pencil. The pen always won. I guess it was stuff like that got me in trouble in the first place, so I tried really hard to resist; at least for that first day.

When class started, we all stood, recited the Pledge of Allegiance, and then it was off to the races as the teacher began to educate our young minds. For one whole hour I sat in class, not hearing much of what the teacher was saying, but just taking in my new surroundings and the joy that was welling up inside me because of them. Of course, it was too good to last. That hour felt like a minute.

After that first class, I had my instructions to return to the Special Ed classroom and this I did with great reluctance. First of all, I was enjoying being a part of a "real" class far too much, but also, I wondered if the other kids would question where I was going and if that would create problems for me.

Fourth grade was when I started becoming more socially aware and conscious of some of the dynamics of cliques, social groups and being "in" as opposed to "out". I was a chunky, quiet kid with a Learning Disability, not a great combination to score high with the popular kids. Still, I wasn't complaining.

Soon enough though, I was questioning whether an hour in the mainstream class had been such a great idea. Some kids had taken notice of my slipping out after the first period and began asking me questions. Also, some of my classmates from third grade had remembered that

I was pulled out of regular classes and so before long, most of my homeroom peers were aware that I was different. I think I was able to hold off most of them by telling them that I was smarter than they were and that I was attending an advanced class. They seemed to accept this explanation and then the following year I transferred to a new school where nobody knew me. Who knows, but I don't think the teasing was quite so ferocious at that age. Little did I know that things could get worse...a lot worse!

◇◇◇◇◇◇◇◇◇◇◇◇◇◇◇◇◇◇◇◇◇◇

Why is it that every Special Ed classroom I have ever gone into is in the most remote part of the school? I guess they don't want the other kids to be infected or something. Or maybe it's that they don't want the normal kids to hear us screaming from the torture. (Just kidding.) Whatever the reason, the Special Ed classroom was always a hard place to find.

> **...they don't want the normal kids to hear us screaming from torture...**

My Special Ed classroom in the fifth grade was by far in the scariest location you could send a kid with a wild imagination. The fact that I was new and didn't know my way around wasn't exactly helpful either. I had hoped with the move to a new town I would shake the Special Ed classroom and the label, but I wasn't that lucky. At least the principal was nice enough to draw me a map.

First, I had to walk outside through the playground.

Then, cross the courtyard and find some long stairs going down. Then at the bottom of the stairwell, I was to go through a thick metal door and turn right. When I opened the metal door, I realized I was now under the school. There were pipes and steam all along the dark hallway leading to the right, and with every step I took I became more and more convinced that someone was watching me. Then, suddenly, a little kid jumped out behind some pipes and said, "I see dead people!" (If you don't know what I'm talking about, check out the movie *Sixth Sense*.)

The last thing I wanted was to be stuck in the dungeon all day long.

Okay... I made up the part about the little kid, but the rest is all true! I was scared out of my mind and kept wondering if I'd taken a wrong turn somewhere and whether I should go back to the principal's office to call my parents to see if it was too late to move back to our old neighborhood. I kept going anyway.

After what seemed like an eternity, I finally came to another door, and knocked. The sound of my knocking echoed throughout the hallway in a horror-movie sound-effect kind of way and I half expected ghosts to start floating through the walls to see who was disturbing their eternal rest.

Finally, the door swung open and a short, older woman popped her head through the opening. I stumbled through my words a little as I nervously introduced myself. She smiled and invited me in. For being in a basement, the room had been decorated quite nicely. The walls were covered with brightly colored posters, and the shelves surrounding the five desks in the middle of the room were lined with games, books and supplies. I met my four new classmates and felt like I was moving up in the world. I started with two classmates and now I had four!

I took my seat and listened to the teacher go over some rules for the year. She seemed nice enough, but despite the bright decorations, and the addition of two more classmates, the room still had that prison-feel to it and I secretly dubbed it "the dungeon". Plus, my new classmates gave me a weird oompa-loompa vibe.

After class was over, the Special Ed teacher sat down with me personally and told me what was expected of me. I was to work hard and communicate my struggles. Then she gave me the best news ever. She told me that I was only expected to spend one hour a day in her classroom, and the remainder of the time I would spend in a mainstream level class.

I was ecstatic! I would have done cartwheels around the classroom had there been room. I figured there must have been some kind of mix up and someone had forgotten to put a cover sheet on her TPS report and the teacher didn't get the memo on how special I truly was. I felt like screaming "FREEEEEEEDOM" but that may have made my teacher a little suspicious (plus the last time William Wallace screamed out that word they cut off his head, and that's just plain gross).

She continued to give me instruction, "You're in Mr. Bovie's class. You will spend most of your day there. You will come down here during your P.E. class and you will bring all your homework and study problems and we will go over them every day so you can stay up with the rest of the class. I am not sure how they ran things at your last school, but our goal is to get you back into the mainstream. If you work hard, you are only required to spend an hour a day with me. If you fall behind, you will be required to spend added time in here. Work hard!"

I thought to myself, "One hour. That's not bad. I can handle that." Things were finally starting to look up. Giving up gym class was an easy sacrifice to make when it meant that I was going to spend the rest of my day in a real, normal classroom. Here I was in a new school with new people that had no idea that I was different, and I was going to do whatever I could to keep it that way.

◇◇◇◇◇◇◇◇◇◇◇◇◇◇◇◇◇◇◇◇◇◇◇◇◇◇

The older I got, the more self-conscious I was of my "handicap", plus I had gotten a few glimpses of how brutal the teasing could get and I did not want to be on the receiving end of such abuse.

For about a month, I did okay. I was hanging in there getting my work done on time, but this was because the first month was mostly review of things the class already knew. When the time came to dig into the new material, I found myself struggling again. I just couldn't keep up. I began to panic. The last thing I wanted was to be stuck in the dungeon all day long.

I quickly decided I had to take drastic measures if I was going to survive. I had to find a way to get my work done, and have it done correctly. And that's how I became a "leech."

A "leech" is a kid who is always asking everyone else for the answers. A leech is the kid who looks over your shoulder when the teacher isn't watching hoping to get a peek at your work.

I also became a cheater. Yep, that's right. I cheated on every test, looked over all the smart kids' shoulders, and begged for every answer.

A "leech" is a kid who is always asking everyone else for answers.

There's no doubt that cheating is wrong for many different reasons, and by no means will I ever say that cheating is okay, (unless you're playing Monopoly with my mega-cheater brother, Chris), but while other kids learned to read better or do their math problems correctly, I was learning to survive. I'm not saying that it was the right thing to do, and I am sure there are much better survival exercises, but when you fear something the way I feared spending more hours in "the dungeon", you know that you have to either sink or swim. If you can't quite figure out how to swim, sometimes the next best option seems to be to tread water.

Looking back, I'm amazed at how much having ADD actually helped me survive my Learning Disability. For a "special" kid, I was pretty darn resourceful. And I didn't mind taking risks. Too bad I didn't use those qualities for something a little bit more honorable than cheating.

I was going to list some of the ways I used these qualities to cheat, but lest I give you any ideas, I'll refrain. Just keep this in mind: As I look back now, I see that going to "the dungeon" would have been the best option, because all the time that I spent cheating, I could have spent learning. Cheating got me nowhere. I still hadn't learned to swim. I was stuck treading water.

There was one particular test that I cheated on that I have to tell you about. I'm sharing this experience more as a way to dissuade any cheaters out there. After I cheated on this test, I was weighed down with guilt like never before.

Oh, and by the way, ADDers love to cling to their guilt. The Bible says that guilt leads to death. Get rid of your guilt and take a step forward. That's what I did after I cheated on this test. I had to because I just couldn't handle the guilt. Let me tell you what happened.

Long ago, I attended a Sunday School called CCD (Christian Catholic Development). The students in the class had to pass a test before they were allowed to go through confirmation. I knew there was no way I could pass that test. Despite the echoing voice in my head saying, "You're going to hell for this one", I still came to class on test day in the middle of July wearing a thick, long-sleeved shirt. The answers had been given to us in the previous class, and while the other students might have used them to study, I made a miniature cheat sheet that I wrapped around my wrist. The only way you could see it was by looking through the gap in the sleeve that was made where I buttoned the cuff.

...he told me that before each test he wanted me to a make a cheat sheet...

I, of course, passed the test but man oh man, did I ever feel guilty for it. I had nightmares of standing at the pearly gates and having Saint Peter say I had to take the test over before he would let me in.

A couple of weeks later, as our CCD class prepared for confirmation, we had to go to confession. Before the priest could even get out, "How long has it been since your last confession," I was begging for forgiveness.

"I cheated on my test! Does God hate me?!? Forgive me!"

Actually, my cheating days were short lived. I got caught. I don't remember what the subject was, but I had everything ready to go so I could ace the test. Once again, I had spent a lot of time preparing a cheat sheet the night before. I had spent hours finding as many answers as I could in the textbook. I then took all the answers and found a way to print them on a small piece of paper. It took some major creativity to fit them all on a piece of paper that small. The next morning, I asked other classmates on the bus ride to school what some of the answers might be. I even asked the teacher (Mr. Bovie) right before the test what some of the answers might be.

Unfortunately, though, I outsmarted myself. I had written the answers in such tiny handwriting that even I couldn't read them. During the test, as I was laboriously trying to decipher my own scribbles, I suddenly realized that Mr. Bovie was standing over me. I looked up to see him, arms crossed over his chest, looking at me rather sternly. He confiscated my cheat sheet and told me to stick around after the test while everyone else went to recess. I thought for sure he would call my parents and I would die that night but instead he looked at my little cheat sheet and said, "Impressive. It looks like it took you some time to do this. It's too bad you didn't spend the time studying."

Wow! Instead of scolding me and dragging me down to

the principal's office, Mr. Bovie took a different approach. First, he praised me for my efforts. I mean, how crazy is that? Here I was cheating on his test and he told me that my cheat sheet was "impressive." I know it sounds nuts! As he scanned the cheat sheet, he noticed that I had almost all the answers to the questions on the test.

"Where'd you get the answers", he asked sternly. I told him that I had gotten them mostly from the book, and then I reminded him of the few answers he had given me just hours ago, before the test. He thought about my answer a moment, then pulled out a test and asked me five random questions. To my great surprise, I got four out of five right.

"Ben, I don't understand why you felt like you had to cheat," he said looking at me with a confused frown. I thought for a moment about how much I should share with him about my struggles. I figured that the fewer people knew about my LD, the better.

Then I thought about how he handled my cheating. He was really cool about it, and I could tell he cared.

So I just came right out and told him that I was having a hard time keeping up, and that the only thing that really mattered to me was being normal. He asked me what I thought would help (aside from cheating). This was the first time a teacher had ever asked me that. In fact, until that day, no one had ever asked me what I thought I needed to do better. They all just made up their minds as to what was best for me.

Mr. Bovie did a lot for me that day. He did not rush in with his own suggestions, but engaged me in the process of creating my own possible solutions. He could have made up his mind as to what he thought would be in my best interest, but instead he listened as I rambled through what I thought could help me overcome my struggles.

We discussed the options, and despite every fiber of my being desperately wanting the opposite, I suggested that I might need a little more time in the Special Ed classroom. I told him that most kids didn't even know there was such a classroom in the school, and if there was any way we could keep it that way, I would be very grateful. Before recess was over, I had laid all my cards on the table.

> ...until that day, no one had ever asked me what I thought I needed to do better...

Mr. Bovie took a few days to think things over. I had dropped quite a bit in his lap. In the end, he came up with a great plan that we both agreed would help solve the problem. The first part of the plan took care of the Special Ed classroom. Apart from attending Special Ed every day during P.E., he made arrangements for me to spend recess in there as well. All the kids were so excited about getting out to play, that they didn't even notice me slipping out to go to class.

Then (and you're not going to believe this one), he told me that before each test he wanted me to make a cheat sheet. He told me that I should do everything I did before to get the answers, but instead of using it, the cheat sheet had to be turned in like an assignment. I thought it was kind of weird at first, but when I started to get decent grades without cheating, I was sold.

All the way through college, I continued to make "cheat sheets" because the process of hunting for the information, writing the information down, and re-reading the information, helped me retain it better.

Mr. Bovie's unconventional approach worked! Instead of writing me off as a cheater and giving me detention like most teachers would have done, he noticed all the hard work and resourcefulness it took for me to put that cheat sheet together. He also knew that my process of finding and then copying the answers might actually cause me to remember the answers.

I finished out fifth grade on a high note, in greater part, I think because I had a learning system in place that catered to my particular needs and struggles - thanks to Mr. Bovie. I had survived my diagnosis for almost two years and I had learned a couple of valuable lessons along the way. I was looking forward to middle school, anticipating that I would continue the same routine and be allowed the same accommodations.

One last note about Mr. Bovie's plan, and it is, by far, the most memorable part. It involved a girl named Stephanie. Mr. Bovie thought it would be good if I had another classmate to help tutor me and keep me accountable. His thought was that I would be more motivated by having another student push me, versus having a teacher push me.

Stephanie was one of the smartest kids in the class, but not only was she smart, she was also cute. I think Mr. Bovie chose Stephanie because she too, was special. Stephanie was a diabetic, and every day, in much the same way I did, she would have to leave class to check her blood sugar levels and get a shot.

When I heard she had to take a shot every day, going to the Special Ed classroom didn't seem so bad. Both of us had a little special something about us so we connected right away. Since Stephanie and I also lived in the same neighborhood, it was easy for us to get a lot of work done. Everything went according to Mr. Bovie's plan until somewhere around the end of that year, one morning, I woke up and realized that I loved Stephanie!

Of course I then did what any crazed-with-puppy-love kid would do; I wrote her the classic two-box note (Will you go out with me? Mark the box, yes or no).

This was the first time I had ever asked a girl to go out with me. I had no idea what to do if she said yes. I didn't know where we were going to go. I just knew that if you liked a girl, you were supposed to ask her to go out with you.

I had slipped her the note in class earlier that day and was on pins and needles to see what her response would be. She gave me the note back before we got on the bus to go home. Instead of opening the note on the bus, I waited until I got home. When the bus dropped me off, I ran all the way home and went straight up to my room. I slammed and locked the door, closed the shades and found a dark corner as if I were looking for a safe place to open a top secret document.

I slowly peeled back the folds of the note, my heart thumping in my chest, and my hands sweaty. To my horror, I noticed she had made her own box below my two boxes. Next to her box she wrote the word, "Maybe." Then, next to that, she wrote, "When you learn to spell." As I looked at the note, I noticed that she had gone through and corrected all of my spelling errors!

The next year, I hoped to show enough improvement in my spelling to woo Stephanie off her feet, but during the summer, her family moved away. In some way, I hope she ends up with a copy of this book and notices that everything is spelled correctly (God bless Spell Check!).

Pep Talk Time

You are a survivor! No matter what anyone says or the struggles you face as you climb the mountains of life, you have what it takes to reach the top. Your adventure will not be a simple walk in the park, but your resourcefulness and creativity will help you find unique and unusual solutions to help you on your way.

I'm not going to tell you that this will be easy; especially when you see others taking what seems to be a smooth and easy route. Not taking the easy way out will strengthen your skills and make you a better and more effective person ready to tackle whatever life throws at you. The key to surviving and reaching the top of any mountain is knowing, not thinking or wondering, not guessing or pondering but knowing you already have everything you need to reach the top.

John Rambo vs John Deere

the Scoop

- It's possible for ADDers to minimize a lot of their struggles
- ADDers notice everything
- ADDers can focus very well
- ADD does not exist in front of a video game

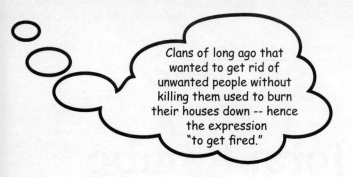

There's a book by Thom Hartmann, called <u>ADD Success Stories</u>. In this book, Hartmann shares a great theory about where ADD characteristics originated. He also explains why these characteristics get such a bad rep in our modern society using a theory he calls the Hunter vs. Farmer. After reading Hartmann's description of "the hunter" and "the farmer", it was easy to see which group I fell into. The ability to notice everything at once, the impulsivity or being able to switch my focus at a moment's notice, the desire for excitement and stimulation, the restlessness, all these qualities would have gotten me a lot of food and leather way back in the day. I'm definitely a Hunter! But, within the regimented, organized and scheduled confines of the modern American school system these characteristics as well as my Dyslexia lead to a diagnosis of LD (and later ADD). Unfortunately, in school, all my Hunter characteristics worked against me.

Isn't it interesting that the clash between ADD qualities

and the behavior expected from a school child became a list of symptoms that is now collectively known as ADHD? Let's just say that today's society likes to reward people who work within the system, rather than those whose primary goal is to go out and fetch their own meat!

Thom Hartmann's theory got me all riled up. I was a Hunter!! How cool is that? Here again was another confirmation that ADD is not just an ordinary disorder where everything about it is negative. It's clear, that given the right environment, ADDers can minimize a lot of their struggles and make full use of their "hunter" qualities in order to lead successful and productive lives.

When I got my official diagnosis in my 20's, I decided to pick the doctor's brain;

"If someone asks me what ADD is, what do I tell them?"

He thought about it for a moment and said,

"Tell them that it's a neurological syndrome that causes things like distractibility, impulsivity, restlessness, procrastination, disorganization, and impatience..." He went on for a bit, but by then I had already tuned him out. All I remember is that he used big words like prefrontal cortex, neurotransmitters, neuroreceptors, and polypeptide bonds. (Okay, I threw in the polypeptide bonds just for fun. It is one of the only words I remember from science class. What can I say? It's a cool word!)

Anyway, those words may offer insight into the science behind the workings of an ADDer's brain and lead to all kinds of stimulating discussions...but only among scientists and doctors. What do those words mean to you? If you're like me, not a heck of a lot! They are just weird sounding words. And what about the summary of symptoms? Being defined by those qualities didn't exactly make me feel like a winner. Is there anybody out there that really wants to be known for being an undisciplined, disorganized, unreliable bobble-head who has a major foot-in-mouth disease? I think not!

> **ADDers can minimize a lot of their struggles and make full use of their "hunter" qualities in order to lead successful and productive lives.**

Still, I knew deep down that there was more to ADD than what the scientific community had made of it. I got tired of hearing the same clichéd explanations and words and took matters into my own hands. (Watch out world!) After I read Hartmann's Hunter vs. Farmer theory, I knew that the Hunter characteristics were great to have... just not in the suburbs of modern America. What bothers me more than anything is that so many of the people I come across - kids, parents, teachers, business professionals - have a lot of misconceptions about ADD. Most people appear to be focused on all the ways that ADD made life difficult for an ADDer and those around them. Very few people recognize that those same qualities, given the right environment and with the right approach, could be an asset to the ADDer and the people closest to them. That's when I started sharing about my ADD more and more.

Recently, I've been thinking about the best way to explain what happens in an ADDer's brain to make us act the way we do, but in non-scientific terms. I came up with a rough illustration that will not stand up to rigorous, scientific scrutiny, but will hopefully help you better understand how brain chemistry affects an ADDer.

In a person's brain, I envision there being a place, much like your favorite hangout, which is really called the pre-frontal cortex. The neurotransmitters (hereafter called skippies – because I really like that name) love to chill out at the hangout. When a bunch of these skippies are at the hangout, a chain reaction occurs giving a person the ability to do a handful of things, including the ability to focus and stay on task.

> The "sparkle" is anything that is interesting, fun, and exciting that catches an ADDer's eye.

Now in a non-ADDer, the skippies like to hang out for quite a while, and even when some of the skippies decide to call it a night and leave, there are still plenty of other skippies hanging out to keep the party going.

In the ADDer's brain, the skippies only like to hang out when something fun is happening. If things get boring, most of the skippies go home. Since the skippies are not at the hangout, there's no chain reaction, and ability to focus is disrupted.

But say the ADDer's scan-the-room-notice-everything super powers pick up something stimulating and interesting going on nearby. Well, a siren goes off that tells the skippies something exciting is going down, and so the skippies come running.

When this happens, an ADDer once again has the

focusing ability. The trick is to utilize the skippies to focus on what's important and not necessarily on what brought those skippies out of hiding. This is where ADD medications like Ritalin come in handy. Ritalin is like a good DJ. He arrives at the hangout and starts spinning some great tunes. Because he's such a fun DJ, the skippies come out and play so long as he's spinning the music.

When the skippies are partying at the hangout an ADDer is able to focus like anyone else. They look intense and engaged. There is no deficit of attention going on. Amazing isn't it?

And here's something else that's pretty wild: Have you ever been around an ADDer who loves to quote movies and knows literally hundreds of quotes? That kind of memorization would be impossible without some intense focusing.

This reminds me of a time when I ate lunch with two brothers named Carl and Justin. We sat around a table eating lemon cake and milk, and between bites, each of us would throw out our favorite movie lines and make the other two guess which movie the quote was from. Both Carl and Justin told me that they have ADD. In fact, Carl wrote a report about "Me and my ADD" for school. Of course he got an A. Way to go Carl!

Anyway, my point is this - how can Carl have ADD and know every other word from the movie, *Anchor Man*? Simple! Carl, Justin, and their ADD friend, Spencer, who, by the way, can eat a pan of lemon cake all on his own, focused really well while they were watching *Anchor Man*. But ask those same guys to give enough attention to the teacher to write down their homework assignments and you might be out of luck. Why? Well, you see this all has to do with this thing I like to call the "sparkle." The "sparkle" is anything that is interesting, fun, and exciting that catches an ADDer's eye. It is the thing that is the most stimulating out of everything else that might be happening around a person with ADD.

The simple fact is that *Anchor Man* sparkles more than math. The skippies are much more interested in a movie than they are in a math class...that's just the way the ADDer's brain works. What can I say; Ron Burgundy is a magnet for attention! The idea of math gets the brain to send out a memo to all the little skippies saying, "Boring! You can find something more stimulating! Keep looking!" That's the simple reason why ADDers have selective attention deficit issues.

I've heard this said of ADD and my own experiences confirm that this is true: The problem lies not in the ability to focus, but in what an ADDer focuses on. I try to share this interesting insight with as many people as I can to help eliminate the misconception that ADDers are people who can't focus at all, on anything. The fact is ADDers can focus very well. We almost have a super-drive focusing mechanism! The issue is that we just don't always have control over where it goes.

One thing about us ADDers is that when we walk into a room, we notice everything. That's right - we see it all. Why? Because our brain is wired to scan the environment for that sparkly thing; we like it when the skippies come out to play!

In the classroom, it's not that we don't want to focus on the teacher; it's just that most of the time, the teacher is not the most interesting (sparkly) thing going on in the room. Or, say we walk into a room that doesn't sparkle either, well, then we ADDers make it sparkle through the use of our very vivid imaginations.

Without something external to get our attention, we will always have to contend with the fact our brains are pulling an Indy 500. We have so many thoughts and ideas zooming through our minds that it's hard to pay attention to anything else going on around us, UNLESS it is more stimulating or sparkly than what's going on inside our own heads.

The problem, therefore, to state it again, is not that ADDers can't focus. The problem is that we focus very well, but mostly on the wrong stuff.

Every time I share this with someone who has ADD or knows someone who does, it is as if a light goes on. Can you imagine being diagnosed with something and being told that you can't focus when you know full well that you can? It can get very confusing.

The fact is that ADDers can focus very well.

I was flying home from a speaking engagement recently. During the flight, the woman sitting next to me decided to start a conversation. As we talked for a few moments, she came to that one question that every person asks when they meet someone new, "So what do you do for a living?"

I told her that I was a motivational speaker and that my platform was the subject of ADD. Of course she asked me if I had taken some classes on the subject and where I got my training. I told her about the books I had read and the classes I took and then I told her that my greatest training had come from the fact that I have ADD. She gave me an odd look and said, "You don't look like someone with ADD."

"What do you think an ADDer should look like?" I asked and watched her face to take on the look of a deer in headlights. She gave me a vibe that she was afraid to offend me. I wondered if she thought that people with ADD were like that neurotic squirrel from the animated movie *Ice Age*. You know, twitchy with an eye tic and a great talent for mass destruction.

"I don't know," she said after a short pause, "I guess you just looked really focused on what you were doing a minute ago."

> **I knew deep down that there was more to ADD than what the scientific community had made of it.**

I gave her one of my more "special" grins, lowered my voice conspiratorially and said, "Let me tell you a little secret. Don't tell anyone, but ADDers can focus. We just act like we can't so we don't have to listen to boring people ramble." I think I scared her or something because she left to go to the bathroom and never came back.

Many people find it hard to believe me when I share this simple explanation of the ADD mind, so I have to prove it further. I share with them the fact that ADD vanishes in front of a Playstation 2. ADD does not exist in front of an X-box, or in front of one of those Nintendo cubie things. Have you ever played one of those games?

They Sparkle, Baby with a capital "S"!!

To me, growing up as a teen in the 80's having access to such video games as Mr. Pacman, Donkey Kong and Galaga, today's games are nothing short of miraculous. I can't even imagine what kind of an impression these games make on my parents and grand-parents, although if my mom is any indication, they become dazed and confused in the mere presence of a game console. One time, mom was over at my house and tried playing one of my Playstation 2 games. She pressed a couple of buttons, the game pad vibrated in her hands, freaked her out, she threw it to the ground and stepped on it. That game pad is dead now (and mom is banned from touching any of my electronic equipment.)

One thing is certain though: between the fast-paced images that pop up onto the screen, the music, and the vibrating game pad, these games are pure ADD candy.

For parents of an ADDer, these games must be a source of great frustration. How can little Johnny spend hours playing Halo or Mortal Combat, yet not be able to complete thirty minutes of homework without literally being tied down to a chair? It's easy to see why some people can come to believe that ADD is nothing more than a discipline issue. (Discipline does play a role, it does in everybody's life regardless of whether they have ADD or not, but it is not the only and the biggest reason why an ADDer's attention tends to wander.) Thankfully, everything starts to fall into place once a person understands that an ADDer's biggest struggle is not with the ability to focus, but with the ability to focus on things that are of no interest to them or offer no stimulation.

So ADDers can focus; now what? Well, it takes some

special manipulating to get us to focus on the right stuff. So there's hope for us you ask? Absolutely.

But the good stuff doesn't stop there. A definition of ADD would not be complete without recognizing another tremendous benefit that comes along with the condition, aside from the extraordinary, if not in this case productive, ability to play Playstation 2 for ten hours straight. With our minds moving at the speed of light - dreaming, scheming, going wild with thoughts - we are wellsprings of great ideas, constantly coming up with a better way to do anything and everything. What ADDers lack in practicality and orderliness, they more than make up for with their vivid imaginations. It has taken me years to understand the great value in this, but I am telling you; we are gifted! We are the type of people who dream big, and dream a lot. Don't underestimate the value of this ability. People who are into organizing, managing and coordinating need us, and value us (if they are smart!). There is tremendous synergistic potential in blending the talents of an ADDer with someone who is strong in the "logistics" department.

One of the biggest challenges ADDers face is finding ways to let our talents and ideas out to shine in all their glory, without losing focus or taking on other destructive habits. This is a tough goal to achieve, but I assure you that with hard work, and a few tricks, which we will discuss in later chapters, you can begin to strengthen your gifts and minimize your challenges.

Pep Talk Time

You knew it all along, didn't you? You knew even when they slapped that label on you that you could pay attention when it mattered...to you! I am sure that as soon as you heard you had something called Attention Deficit Disorder, you thought the same thing I did: Something is not adding up.

If I can pay attention and focus on things I find interesting, why are they giving me a label that is going to lead everyone to believe I can't? Remember this one thing: Labels come and go, so don't get hung up on yours. Did you know that Attention Deficit/Hyperactivity Disorder started out being known as "Defect of Moral Control"? Yikes! Also, at one point, the scientists thought that children with ADD were brain damaged! Let's face it - the jury is still out on ADD. Who knows, in a few years they might discover that ADDers are all geniuses!

Whether or not anyone ever figures out the science behind ADD, you need to know that there are multiple benefits from possessing those "Hunter" characteristics. Most people don't get to walk into a room and notice everything like you do. You have more ideas in one day than most people have in a year! Your ADD is more than a "gift" – it's a POWER! And like Peter Parker (Spiderman's) uncle said, "With great power comes great responsibility." In order to take full advantage of the Power, you will need to accept the responsibilities of learning to manage and control that Power within you. So get past the label and step up to the plate!

"There aren't any icons to click. It's a chalk board."

The "X" Factor

the Scoop

- Not all teachers understand ADD
- School buses are today's version of the gauntlet - not every kid survives

Did you know that there are coffee flavored PEZ?

Sixth grade brought many changes into my life. I was starting on the bottom rung of a new, bigger school. There was no Stephanie, and there was also no Mr. Bovie there to support my fragile self-esteem and fledgling success. I knew some of the kids from my old school, but there was a far greater number of unfamiliar faces. I did my best to stay positive, but of course I was very nervous. Would I make new friends? Would my homeroom teacher be nice? And what about my Special Ed status? What were they going to do with me this year?

It wasn't long before they rounded up all the "special" kids and put us through a day of testing. I went to take the tests hoping against hope that I would do well enough to slide into a regular schedule. This was of course wishful thinking. After they scored the tests, it was determined that I still needed the extra attention of a Special Ed program. The way the schedule worked out, I was going to be splitting my time between Special Ed and mainstream-level classes. And so, I found myself in yet another Special Ed classroom.

Thankfully, this classroom was located above ground, and had a window! So, on day three of Junior High, I walked in and met my new Special Ed instructor.

In the book, Answers to Distraction, by Dr. Edward M. Hallowell and Dr. John J. Ratey, the authors share about a time when a teacher at Phillips Exeter Academy was asked to answer the question, "What's a learning disability?" The teacher answered by saying, "There are two kinds of learning disabilities: one treatable, the other not. The treatable one is laziness, and the untreatable one is stupidity."

She never came right out and called us "dumb" to our faces, but we knew how she felt about us by the way she treated us.

It's unfortunate, but there are still, even with all the information available, many teachers who feel the same way about learning disabilities. In sixth grade, I was unfortunate enough to encounter one such teacher. I do remember her name, but for the purposes of this book, I will simply refer to her as Mrs. X.

Now a lot of people don't know this about me, but I actually went to college to be a teacher. I went through all the classes and even did some clinicals. As I went through my education classes in college, I noticed that there were two types of students. There were the students who had a true passion and desire to teach and make a difference in young peoples' lives. Then there were the students who simply wanted their summers off.

Mrs. X was a teacher who wanted her summers off. I say that because that's what she told the class. I remember that first day when she addressed us. There were three of us there, and she said, "Okay guys. Let's do what we can so we can make it to summer."

Apparently, she fell into the Special Ed program because that was what was available when the school was hiring. She told us that as well. If you were to walk into the Special Ed classroom, you could tell that it reeked of joy, enthusiasm and passion…. NOT!

Mrs. X really didn't want to be there and she really shouldn't have been there. She hadn't worked with Special Ed students before and it showed every day through her actions and the things she would say.

If I was at all ahead when I entered the sixth grade, I soon lost ground. The first week of class, Mrs. X made me take a bunch of additional tests: I felt I was doing well, but Mrs. X would make disparaging comments about some of my answers. For three days, I tested in her class, and with each passing day, I felt more and more stupid. She never came right out and called us "dumb" to our faces, but we knew how she felt about us by the way she treated us.

My self-esteem was a fragile thing (still is), and it didn't take much to crush it. Every hour I spent in that classroom, my self-esteem dwindled, sucked dry by the one person who was supposed to be helping me. I can't tell you if she did it intentionally, or if she just didn't know how to speak to a Special Ed student. But her actions seemed brutal. She would tell us that our answers were stupid. She would tell us that we did dumb things, and her idea of encouragement was to tell us to work hard because right now, none of us would make it in a mainstream level class. I guess she thought that she had to be cruel to be kind. Too bad she didn't know that cruelty and disparagement is one approach that NEVER works with us ADDers.

...cruelty and disparagement is one aproach that NEVER works with us ADDers...

During my first two full years of being a Special Ed student, I was forced to deal mostly with the way I felt about myself. There was some sporadic teasing from kids, but by and large my parents and teachers were supportive and encouraging. Now I was in uncharted waters. I had never had a teacher make me feel the way this teacher did. It is one thing to have a classmate put you down, but when a teacher, an adult, the one person who is supposed to be helping you, puts you down, it's a whole different kind of a wound.

To make matters worse, one day, when I got up to leave my homeroom class to go to Special Ed, someone actually paid attention to my slipping out and asked the teacher where I was going.

"Oh, Ben has a special class that he needs to attend." the teacher said without so much as a pause. My heart stopped beating! She had just exposed my secret in front of the entire class! I shut the door behind me quickly as every student turned to look at me exiting when they heard the word "special." I didn't hear any more of the discussion if there was one, but I feared it would have something to do with the word "stupid." As I walked to the Special Ed classroom, my heart was sinking; the hope I had of being normal and fitting in began evaporating and I was suddenly afraid. Afraid of what all those kids would say to me and to each other now that they knew that I had "special" classes. By then I knew what happened to kids who were different and it wasn't pretty. I tried to steel myself for the bus ride home, hoping that between second period and the end of the day, the kids would have forgotten all about me.

No such luck.

Picture it for a moment: thirty or so kids, hopped up on sugary cereals or snacks, jammed into a cramped space. Nothing good can ever come of that. Unless the bus is fitted with shackles and chains, kids are bouncing off their seats either from the pound of sugar they have consumed only minutes before boarding the bus or simply because they are glad to be done with school for the day.

Riding that school bus was almost... no, it was the ugliest imaginable experience for me. That banana boat on wheels turned out to be a mobile torture chamber. I think what made it worse is that I could never predict how each ride would turn out. One day, I would be left alone and then the next, it was as though there was a wanted sign posted somewhere with my mug on it and everyone was showing up to get a piece of the action.

Sure, there was the bus driver, but he or she was usually tied up with the driving, their number one goal to just get the out-of-control shipment of kids to and from the school as fast as possible in one piece. Most of the time, the drivers just turned up the radio and ignored what was going on behind them. Maybe once in a blue moon the bus driver would look up into that huge mirror and give us a long hard stare, but that was about it. Then as soon as his eyes were back on watching the road, spitballs went flying, heads got smacked, and of course, the teasing and name-calling would resume. I'm sure not much has changed in this regard in the last twenty years.

I hated getting any kind of attention on that bus because it was never good. Thinking back, had the movie *Speed* been out then, I probably could have related to those poor people being stuck on a bus, held hostage by a madman who would not be satisfied until I was blown to bits.

When I got on the bus that afternoon, it actually wasn't too bad at first. I had a chance to sit down before someone asked me the first question. "Yeah dude, what's wrong with you?"

I had worked all day to find the right answer but I still didn't know what to say.

"Why do you have to go to a special class?" another kid asked.

I wanted so badly to respond with my usual, "I'm smarter than you" story, but instead I froze up from pure self-consciousness. These kids were older than me and I sensed that they weren't going to believe me anyway. Their minds were already made up. So I just sat there, stared at my feet and said nothing. Then it started…the name-calling: Stupid, Idiot, Moron, Loser. The grand finale to all the verbal abuse was of course the humiliation of having my head slammed against the bus window.

That day, the kids who were somehow "in charge" of this

merciless task declared me an outsider, an undesirable, and an unwanted and unwelcome presence on that bus. And those kids were not shy about letting me know what they thought of me. I became the target because I was different.

When the bus finally got to my stop and the doors opened, I ran home, went straight to my room, and cried. It was at this point I began to pray, "God, why me?! Why do I have to be the special kid?" That was one of the worst days of my life and I relived it, with some variations, for the rest of the sixth grade.

There are days when I wish I could go back in time and tell those cruel children all the things I know now about learning disabilities and ADD, just to try and help them understand this common struggle. The last I heard, Doc Brown crashed into the time machine with a train. So unless you know where I can pick up a time machine, I'm out of luck.

But at least I can get the word out today. It might help you the next time you're on a school bus.

If I were on that bus today and someone asked me what was wrong with me, I'd tell them, "Back off, I'm Special and I'm not afraid to use it!"

Then I would let them figure out the rest.

Pep Talk Time

*Some days are harder than others, aren't they? I know
sometimes you have some really rough days, days where
maybe you are thinking about throwing in the towel and
giving up on yourself and your life. I know how you feel.
Believe me, I had those days myself and let me tell you,
I'm glad that they are behind me. But more importantly,
I'm glad that somehow, by the Grace of God, I was able
to get through that time without doing anything self-
destructive like turning to violence, drugs or worse.
As you read this, I need you to keep something very
important in mind: This too shall pass! I didn't come
up with that line, but it is a powerful and profound
statement that you need to memorize and repeat to
yourself every time, something unpleasant is happening
to you. This too shall pass. You will not be in this
situation for the rest of your life. In fact, even a few
short months from today, you and your life can be
in a totally different place on one condition: You are
proactive in changing your life and your attitude. Sit
there and do nothing you'll probably keep going around
in circles in the same prison cell, but stretch yourself
and look for opportunities to do, think, act, react,
speak and listen differently and you will be amazed
at how much your life will change...for the better!*

9
Putt-Putt Benny

the Scoop

- Fred Flintstone vitamins can only do so much
- Negative emotions, like anger and anxiety, can be bad for your health if not dealt with properly
- The most distracting thing for an ADDer is a negative thought

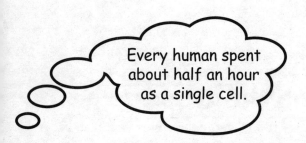

The uncertainty I felt when I entered sixth grade had become fully justified. I was living in a nightmare. The more I thought about my situation, the more hopeless it seemed. I once heard someone give this illustration about hope and it makes a lot of sense: There were two mice that were placed into two separate buckets of water. The test was to find out how long each mouse could tread water before drowning. I know, I know, terribly cruel, but nevertheless, the outcome was interesting. One of the mice tread water for just 30 minutes, while the other mouse tread water for something like eight hours. What was the difference between the two rodents? It wasn't their size, age or health status. The biggest difference was that the mouse that tread water for eight hours was taken out of the water for ten seconds every twenty minutes or so; the other mouse was never taken out at all. One explanation for such a huge difference in endurance was simply that the surviving mouse had hope while the other did not.

By the middle of 6th grade, I had lost all hope of being normal, and, like the mouse that didn't make it, I began to give up. My attitude was bad, my work was poor, and I couldn't remember the last time I "made the fridge".

Part of the problem was that I felt like I had no options. There were no choices to make - everything had been decided for me. No one asked me if I wanted to be 'special". No one asked if I wanted to attend Special Ed. No one asked if the way I was being taught by Mrs. X. was helpful to me. The only person, Mr. Bovie, who'd given me any kind of choice was out of my life and

I felt like I had no options.

now on top of everything, I had to deal with the huge social implications of being the "special kid".

I felt trapped. As far as I could tell, my future was set. I was disabled, abnormal, different and therefore unlovable and without the possibility of ever making friends or amounting to anything. My one daydream as a kid was that I could be like Arthur Fonzarelli, also known as The Fonz from the show *Happy Days*. The Fonz was the coolest guy to ever walk the planet! He snapped his fingers and the rest of the world came running. I used to like to pretend to be him, snapping my fingers, turning up the collar of my coat, then sticking up my thumbs and saying "Heeeyyy." After a few weeks of those bus rides I couldn't even summon up the energy to do my Fonz impersonation in the privacy of my own bedroom, much less in front of the kids in the lunchroom. Who was I kidding? The Fonz was a genius and what was I exactly? A big nothing. A mistake. A loser. I was feeling lower than low, do you really think I cared how I did in class?

Before the end of that year, my parents had been called in many times about my lack of improvement, but yet, what could they do?

My mother knew that something was wrong, and every day I came home she would ask how things were going. I could never find the words to tell her that I felt that my life was one big "ugly" and I wished that I could start over. It would have been nice if the best part of the game of golf could be applied in life; it's called a mulligan. My good friend Phil (who needs to use a mulligan on almost every hole) taught me that any time you hit a really bad shot in golf, all you have to do is call it a "mulligan," and you get to hit the golf ball again.

I really wanted to start over. I wanted to go back to the way things were before "the tests." And I prayed that God would give me a different life or let me start fresh. What I learned is that life doesn't offer do-overs. Occasionally, you'll hear about some miraculous escape from death that someone experiences or a medical miracle wherein a person gets a "second chance," but for the most part, we have to do what we can with what we've got. And that includes the ugly stuff.

All the progress and achievements from the previous two and a half years of Special Ed seemed to have vanished. I had lost the confidence that I built up. Why? Simply because I was starting to believe all that trash I was hearing on the bus and in that Special Ed classroom every day. I wasn't sure how to tell my mom about this. I felt like a loser and I figured that my parents wouldn't like me very much either if they knew their son was a loser. Besides, what could they do to help?

On the ride home, after one of those little "meetings", my mother would not leave me alone, "What's the problem? What's going on with you? Tell me what you're thinking!"

I really wanted to tell her how I felt. I wanted to share all about the hellish bus rides I had to endure twice a day, but I just couldn't. There were all these thoughts rushing through my mind about how I felt, and why I felt that way, and what could or could not be done about it. I just didn't know where to start, so instead I gave her the old stand-by, "I don't know." After that, I just kept silent until she quit bugging me.

Sometime around April, I woke up, and it was as if all the hurt and pain came crashing down upon me, and I was unable to move. For almost three weeks, I stayed home, sick. No one could figure out what was wrong with me, not even our family doctor. Mom's magic chicken broth wasn't helping and I was definitely beyond the scope of the healing power of Fred Flinstone Vitamins. I was like Humpty Dumpty - no one could put me back together again. (By the way, I hated Fred Flintstone vitamins. Maybe they have improved them since I was a kid, but back then, those things were downright nasty. They were the

What I learned is that life doesn't offer do-overs.

worst tasting vitamins ever. It was like eating dried-up Tang chunks. I used to have this little chalkboard desk that had drawers that were meant to hold magnetic letters and numbers that would stick to the chalkboard. When my mom felt that I had grown out of this toy, she decided to put it in a garage sale. When she opened the drawers to see if all the number and letters were still intact, she found a small fortune in Fred Flintstone vitamins. That thing was jam-packed! My mom was so mad she almost made me eat every last one of those tablets there and then.)

After I missed about two weeks of school, my mom was getting desperate. She finally decided to take me to a traditional Chinese doctor. I can remember going into a tiny, cluttered store, filled with all kind of bizarre items. Statues of Buddha perched high on crooked shelving, bundles of herbs hanging from the ceiling, cans with Chinese writing on them, some brightly colored, satin-looking robes and slippers in one of the corners and a multitude of other fascinating items that I didn't have time to take in. It smelled funny in there too.

We got ushered into a back room by a tiny Chinese woman. I didn't know what to expect, but there was the standard exam table, a desk and a chair. I sat on the table and my mom sat in the chair. I was nervous, expecting to get a shot, or worse yet, one of those super-sized Q-tips doctors love, jammed down my throat. Instead, this old Chinese guy had me stick out my tongue, which he studied intently for what felt like ten minutes. Then he looked at my eyeballs, pulling down my lower lids much more than I found comfortable. He also looked at my hands, pinching the skin in several places on my arms. Through all this, I could hear my stomach making weird, gurgling noises, which was kind of embarrassing. The last thing the Doctor did was feel my stomach, pressing down here and there and at one point actually putting his ear to my belly and listening for a few moments. You should have seen my mom's face – I think she was having second thoughts about bringing me to this guy! He performed a couple of other "tests", all the while talking to himself in Chinese, then he looked at my mom, and said, "Your son has gas."

That's right folks, he said "GAS!"

My mom has the best expressions, and I will never forget the way her face twitched when she heard the word "gas." I am sure she was expecting the worst, but being diagnosed with gas was almost comical. I could tell that she was relieved, but also very confused. "How can gas make a kid this sick?" she asked.

The Doctor did his best to explain that it looked like I had recently been under some major stress and that I had bottled up all my anxiety and that this was the likely reason why I was having all the cramps and pain in my stomach. He said that negative emotions like anger, anxiety, frustration, fear and others can be a dangerous thing if not dealt with properly. He then turned to me and told me that I needed to find a way to relieve the stress inside me or that stress would continue to take a toll on my health.

> ...I was like Humpty-Dumpty - no one could put me back together again...

I had no idea that being stressed out and anxious could make me that sick! It's amazing how we can hurt ourselves without really being aware of it.

There is a movie called *My Life* staring Michael Keaton which has a similar situation to the one I am sharing about myself. There was a kid who grew up with all kinds of problems. He wasn't labeled "special," but had a hard time all the same. He spent many years beating himself up. As an adult character played by Michael Keaton, the young boy who abused himself with "stinking thinking" finds out that he has cancer. He and his wife desperately try to find a cure, but nothing works. All appears lost.

Finally, the character is willing to try anything, and ends up in an unconventional doctor's office. Without any needles or super-sized Q-tips, the doctor discovers the cause of the cancer - unresolved, built-up stress, anger, hurt, and pain.

Now I know that this was just a movie but it sure hit home with me when I saw this film as an adult.

Can stress kill you? Maybe not outright, but studies show that the presence of persistent stressors in our lives cause anxiety, decrease our ability to fight off bacterial and viral infections, and if present in someone's life long enough, cause exhaustion so severe that the person can't even get out of bed. That was me!

The more I think about it, the more it makes sense. If you speak death and hate and pain into your life, what do you think the results are going to be? Negative. If you speak hope and joy and happiness, what do you think the results may be? Positive.

The problem was that I was under a dual attack: From my peers, who hated the fact that I was not like them, and from myself, as I began believing their words and spent most of my waking moments beating up on myself. I needed to stop abusing myself, first and foremost, and then I would have a chance to get better.

Someone once asked me at a speaking engagement,

"What is the greatest distraction for an ADDer?" It took me no time at all to think of the answer. I knew it all too well. The greatest distraction we ADDers face is a negative thought.

Earlier, I told you that when an ADDer walks into a room, he or she will notice everything, and it is the most sparkly thing in the room (to them) that the ADDer focuses on.

Well now let's say there was something in that room that was absolutely ugly. What do you think would have more draw: the sparkly or "the ugly"? I wish I could say that the positive, uplifting sparkle would win my focus, but something ugly will always win over something sparkly. "The ugly" in the room is much like a train wreck - I want to look away, but I just can't.

Why is that? I think even non-ADDers struggle with this, but for us ADDers, it's twice as bad. Must. Look. At. Nasty. Gory. Accident. Can't. Look. Away. Our most dangerous distractions come in the form of the "ugly." And most of the time that "ugly" is a negative thought.

Do you remember the last time someone really got under your skin? How long did you spend obsessing about the situation?

If you're anything like me, when you experience something negative, like an argument or hearing that someone's been saying bad things about you behind your back, you have the hardest time letting it go. An ADDer's mind has a tendency to become consumed with the situation. Millions of thoughts and emotions bombard us, stimulating us to the point where we become hyper-focused on the issue even if in the grander scheme of things it is fairly insignificant. We submerge ourselves in an emotional whirlwind that looks like this:

Why do they think I'm a jerk?
What did I do to them?
They're the jerk!
Is it possible that I'm a jerk?
I wonder if anyone else thinks I'm a jerk?
I know that so and so thinks I'm a jerk!
Maybe I am a jerk!
I didn't even do anything! Or did I?
What did I do to make them think I'm a jerk?
Is there something I can do to change their mind?

You get the idea.

Everyone, regardless of whether they are ADD or not, go through situations where they get caught up in this kind of mind frenzy, but ADDers are particularly susceptible. I have tried explaining to non-ADDers the intensity with which we experience negative thoughts. I would almost equate it with possession. Nothing else matters. We can't focus on anything else, we can't sleep, we don't enjoy our meals or interactions with other people. All energy is directed to the thing that bothers us the most. Imagine thousands of thoughts and ideas passing through our brain, influencing our actions and attitudes. Imagine, for a moment, that many of these thoughts are negative and self-destructive. Scary, isn't it?

> **I had no idea that being stressed out and anxious could make me that sick!**

When I was growing up, my older brother, trying to be funny, would come up to me once in a while, put his nose right up to my mouth take a long sniff, make a face, and say, "Dude, you must be hating yourself. Your breath stinks!"

He was just being a jerk, but he may have had a point. I had been sitting on the bus every day for almost a year and every day it seemed that someone would call me a name. And even though, bit-by-bit, people lost interest and got bored with teasing me, I still found myself feeling worse and worse. Why? Because long after others stopped mocking me, I was still mocking myself. I ended up being harder on myself than anyone else. Not my parents, not my teacher and not even the mean kids said the negative, hurtful things to me that I said to myself.

> **Not my parents, not my teacher and not even the mean kids said the negative, hurtful things to me that I said to myself.**

If you've seen the movie *Liar, Liar,* you might remember the scene where the Jim Carrey character, Fletcher Reede, beats himself up in the men's bathroom. He bangs his head on the sink, slams himself into the wall, and punches himself in the face (all to just get out of being in court). In the middle of this self-beating, some guy comes in and witnesses the character's bizarre behavior. In shock, the stranger asks, "What are you doing?"

And Fletcher Reede says, "I'm kicking my own butt! Do you mind?"

ADDers can kick their own butts with the best of them. Along with being impulsive, distracted, disorganized, and impatient, one of our biggest struggles is low self-esteem.

Somewhere between sixth grade and high school, I fully mastered the art of negative inner dialogue. All the questions I had the first couple of years after being diagnosed had been asked and answered. Too bad these answers were mostly inaccurate. So I learned to listen to the negative voice inside of me. And because the sound of my own voice was familiar to me, I trusted it. It took a long time to realize that sometimes that particular little voice needs to be told to shut it! Actually, and please don't think that they should add schizophrenia to my diagnosis, I believe that we all have two different and distinct voices inside of us vying for our attention; One voice is the voice of reason, the one that addresses us telling us that everything will be okay and that we've got potential and something to live for. The other voice is the one always dragging us down, telling us that we're no good, that we'll never make it, to quit, to throw in the towel and that life stinks. What happened to me is that after hearing so much external negativity, I chose to only listen to the negative voice. The voice of reason was still inside of me, I just ignored it.

I didn't know then, and even now sometimes I forget, how powerful words can be. The Bible tells us that God spoke the world into existence and even if you don't believe that, you'll know that without words, we'd be unable to communicate, to pass down knowledge, to share our memories and experiences, to express our emotions, or do much of anything else that requires us to interact with another human being. Words are powerful like nothing else.

Imagine the damage a million negative words recited internally can do to a person. It's like an internal atomic bomb ticking! No wonder I got sick. I was speaking death into my body every time I told myself I was no good, stupid, or worse.

Words are a powerful thing and we should be more

careful about how we use them. I heard someone once say we need to be in the "build-Ben-up" business versus the "tear-him-down" business. I needed to change my inner dialogue. I needed to get into the "build-Ben-up" business.

As my mom and I headed home from the doctor's office that day, she told me in the best way she knew how that I was the cause of my own sickness. I had only one choice and that was to learn to let things out and to let them go. I had to change my destructive thinking to a positive response.

◇◇◇◇◇◇◇◇◇◇◇◇◇◇◇◇◇◇◇◇◇◇◇◇

I wish I could tell you that the visit with the Chinese doctor gave me the necessary motivation to change the way I viewed my situation and the reality of not being like everyone else. Fact was, I was just too young to apply the wisdom he shared with me and I was too consumed by my need to fit in and be accepted. I couldn't explain it, but I "knew" that it was vitally important that I have friends and now it seemed as if the whole world had turned its back on me. I might as well have been shuttled to the cold, dark, empty surface of the moon, dropped off with a small backpack of supplies and told, "Good luck, buckaroo!"

The reality is that every day, kids everywhere wake up and look forward to their day because of the companionship and the fun that they will experience due to friendships. Take that away and it's hard to get out of bed. I knew that first-hand. It hurt to see other kids huddled together laughing and looking like they belonged and to be the outsider. I was tired of being left out.

◇◇◇◇◇◇◇◇◇◇◇◇◇◇◇◇◇◇◇◇◇◇

Let's face it - no one enjoys being lonely. I feared loneliness so much that I preferred to be around people I didn't like, doing things I shouldn't have been doing, rather than be alone.

I used to get confused, and think that being lonely meant that I was inferior, or unlikable. Really, it often meant that I was so different that no one else really "got" me. Being that different was actually a big, undiscovered gift, but it took me a long time to realize this.

In school, I thought everyone should want to be like the cool kids. But looking at the situation from where I am now, it's obvious that being "different" can be the best thing in the world. Of course if you're the "special" kid, you're probably thinking that I'm crazy for saying that, but you have to trust me on this one.

Sometimes I wonder if God looks down on us and scratches his head at how much energy we all expend on being the same as everyone else. Diversity is a wondrous, wonderful thing.

I believe that a creative and loving God crafted each of us and that each person is a priceless masterpiece. I only wish that we were better at recognizing our own value.

When I began to get over my own fears and insecurities, I was able to focus on developing my gifts and talents instead of beating myself up for my short-comings. This slow change in my attitude ultimately saw me make friends with an eighty-year old man who opened the door to my future as a speaker and chalk artist. It was an opportunity I would have missed, if I was still caught up in trying to be like everyone else.

Pep Talk Time

"You must strive to find your own voice. Because the longer you wait to begin, the less likely you are to find it at all. Thoreau said, 'most men lead lives of quiet desperation.' Don't be resigned to that. Break out!" (Dead Poets Society) Dump the idea that there are normal people and special people, and discover the truth that there are only unique people. Being given a label is simply getting to have a little more uniqueness than others. When you learn to see yourself as special, rather than "special" with the quotation marks, you can start to appreciate your own value and the fact that you have a lot to offer to the world. A whole lot! Will you go through lonely times? Yes. Can you survive those and come out on the other side better and stronger than ever? Most definitely, but there's a catch; Don't waste any time feeling sorry for yourself and hating life. This is something that YOU have total control over. Every morning when you wake up, you get to decide what mood you're going to be in that day. Choose to be positive! Choose to put a smile on your face. Choose to live life to the fullest!

10

Dear Teacher...

the Scoop

ADD is real!

"When do they take us out to go to the bathroom?
I don't think I can hold it much longer!"

Every year, I speak to hundreds of teachers and educators and I love seeing the light go on for many of them when I share some of the basic facts about ADD and working with ADD students. Most teachers hunger for information that's practical and relevant to their day-to-day dealings with "special" students. There's at least one in every classroom and ADD is widespread enough that all teachers should be equipped to deal with students who have it!

Unfortunately, there are no mandatory classes about ADD that teachers have to take and as a result every school has teachers like Mrs. X., my sixth grade Special Ed. teacher who made no secret of the fact that she thought we were a bunch of dummies.

If you're a teacher reading this, here's what your ADD students need you to understand: ADD is real! Whether or not it can be considered a legitimate disorder and whatever the scientists decide to call it next, there are people out there who possess a combination of certain, specific characteristics that ultimately labels them as ADD. These characteristics include such things as impulsivity, hyperactivity, inattention, and disorganization on the one hand and creativity, resourcefulness, perceptiveness, great imagination, and fearlessness on the other. ADDers are also known for having high IQ's.

ADDers love nothing more than to bring a smile to your face, to get recognition, acceptance, to make you happy.

In their book Answers to Distractions, Dr. Edward M. Hallowell and Dr. John J. Ratey exhort ADDers to keep the following in mind: "Remember that what you have is a neurological condition. It is genetically transmitted. It is caused by biology, by how your brain is wired. It is not caused by a weakness in character, or by a failure to mature. Its cure is not to be found in the power of the will, nor in punishment, nor in sacrifice, or in pain. Always remember this: Try as they might, many people with ADD have great trouble accepting the syndrome as being rooted in biology rather than weakness of character."

Having experienced this first-hand, I believe that the reason so many ADDers suffer from low self-esteem is because parents and teachers do not adequately affirm the fact that ADD is a biological phenomenon and not one of moral conduct. ADDers need to hear that they are not lazy or crazy or stupid.

With that in mind, please load your ADD students

up with lots of praise and encouragement. Will there be discipline cases, disguised as ADD in your care at one point or another? Most likely there will be, but by and large, those kids in your class who twitch and fiddle and talk out of turn and doodle and daydream are the potential future artists, movie stars, inventors, musicians, entrepreneurs and motivational speakers. Yes, they are disruptive and often annoying in class and there are days when you want to choke the life out of them, but keep in mind that most of us ADDers would love nothing more than to bring a smile to your face, get recognition, be accepted and to make you happy. We're not great at seeing things through, but if you take the time to learn how to handle us, we will, no doubt, be some of your most memorable and possibly, best liked students.

"Class, who can tell me what I have preserved in this jar?
No, it's not a pig or a baby cow...it's the last student
who got caught cheating on one of my tests!"

11

Impulsivity:
Fire!
Ready!
Aim?

the Scoop

- Impulsivity may be the most challenging of all ADD characteristics
- "How-I-feel-right-now" decisions are usually the wrong decisions
- Seek productive partnerships

If you have
3 quarters, 4 dimes, and
4 pennies, you have $1.19. You
also have the largest amount of
money in coins without being
able to make change
for a dollar.

Of all the traits that ADD bestows on the person born with the "disorder", I think "impulsivity" is the one quality that has the potential to be the most misunderstood and destructive. And that is why I'm dedicating a full chapter to it!

Impulsivity is one big reason why ADDers have a knack for getting into all kinds of trouble. We have a tendency to consistently do the opposite of what we say and think we want to do and also what we know is the appropriate thing to do in the moment. This is a huge area of frustration for us. It reminds me of a passage in the Bible where the Apostle Paul asks, "Why do I do what I know I shouldn't do, and why don't I do what I should do?" (Romans 7:19)

If you're like me, when you do the opposite of what you should, it is not because you enjoy "being difficult" and testing the patience of those around you! The fact is, you just can't help yourself. You get so caught up in an idea that you fail to stop and think about the consequence of your actions if you follow through on your impulse. One of the best things you can do for yourself is learn how to control your impulsivity.

Here's a little story I made up that I like to share with people when I try to explain what being impulsive means. Let's say there are three kids sitting on the roof of a two story building. One of the three kids has ADD. One of the "normal" kids starts joking around and asks, "If we jumped off this building, how many times do you think we would bounce?" The other "normal" kid looks over the edge and notices

> **Whatever we feel like doing right now, we have a tendency to do right now.**

that it's a long way down. His brain kicks in and he says, "I don't think we should jump. It looks like a long way down. Besides there are thorn bushes down there!" In the meantime, the kid with ADD, well, he's already on his second bounce! I'm sure you're thinking what I'm thinking... Break out the Band-aids!

Being impulsive, to me, means that the little voice in our brain that's supposed to be screaming STOP! (Or POTS! if you're dyslexic) is usually silent or simply speaks up too late to prevent the mischief. Remember the old *Tom and Jerry* cartoon where Tom has a chance to smash snoozing Spike's head (the big, mean bulldog) with a cast iron pan? Before he swings the pan down onto Spike's melon, two mini-Toms appear on each of his shoulders. One mini-Tom has red horns and a pitchfork, and looks much like a devil, and the other mini-Tom has wings and a halo, and looks like an angel. The devil mini-Tom is screaming, "Do it! Do it!" The angel mini-Tom is yelling, "No, no!" In the end, the devilish mini-Tom wins and the skillet ends up smashed over Spike's head, and, of course, Tom pays dearly for this. To me, being impulsive is like having two little devils on my shoulders egging me on and no one to yell, "STOP"!

Being impulsive also leads to a lot of How-I-Feel-Right-Now-At-This-Moment decisions. Whatever we feel like doing right now, we have a tendency to do right now. There is no pausing to consider how these actions might affect others. It's not a lack of consideration, but the fact that the desire to fulfill the impulse is stronger than anything else. Why? Because the impulse captures our focus, creates a "hyper-focused" state where everything else going on around us fades into the distant background becoming muffled and unimportant in that moment.

This is a Now/In-The-Moment decision:
I think it now-- I say it now!
I want it now-- I buy it now!
I don't like you now-- I dump you now!
I don't like my job now-- I quit my job now!
I feel like it now-- I do it now!

You get the idea.

Does self-discipline play a role in this aspect of an ADDer's behavior? Yes. With time, if you work on it, you'll be able to exert a greater influence over yourself. There is also no question that what we are dealing with is a significant impulse control issue. You know that even in the middle of a test, it's going to be very hard to stop yourself from telling everyone else that the man mowing the lawn outside the classroom window is wearing frayed Daisy Dukes, no shirt and has a hairy Sasquatch-looking back...well, okay, I don't think that I could stop myself...

So let's review what we know: ADDers selectively focus. ADDers are impulsive. ADDers desire to do well.

I believe one of the keys to combating this issue is learning to partner up with people who do not have ADD; seek productive partnerships in all aspects of your life: school, work, family and love. Then, as a team, look for creative ways that you can let each other's talents shine. You will be amazed how much you can achieve and how much fun you can have. It'll make you forget all about the Sasquatch outside your window.

Unfortunately, it is not always easy to find the right people to be on your team, but they are out there. And while you're keeping your eye out for these individuals, learn to acknowledge and recognize your own impulsivity. Slow down. Stop. Count to ten. Think.

Pep Talk Time

It's not because we're lazy. It's not because we have a major problem with discipline. It's not because we're trying to make someone mad. It's because we're impulsive. I know that a lot of stunts we pull, we don't do with the idea of hurting anyone. It's just our brain trying to entertain itself. However, being impulsive does not mean we get an automatic "get out of jail free" card. One truth that will always stand the test of time is the fact that there will always be consequences for our actions. Right now, there are thousands of ADDers like you and me sitting in jail because they had an impulsive moment. As nice as it would be to pull out a card that says, "Please excuse Ben from all his actions today; he's special;" it will never happen.

So the only choice we have is to take the right action. In the same way a poor decision leads to a negative outcome, the right decision will lead to a positive outcome. Like I said, every action has a consequence, so why can't that consequence be positive?

The first "right" action you need to take is to accept the fact that you are impulsive. The positive outcome from this is that you will become more self-aware.

When you begin to identify the areas in your life where you are the most impulsive, you can begin to take steps to help avoid those situations. If your brain has a tendency to go off when you're sitting next to the window, you can move your desk. If you know sitting next to the BD kid named Bob will cause you to be impulsive, then you can ask to change seats. Becoming more self-aware is not an easy thing to do, but just recognizing the difficulty of it empowers you to begin taking baby steps in the right direction.

And don't rely on just yourself. Ask others to assist you, and hold you accountable. Who better than the people around you to help you identify those moments when you are doing something you don't want to do? Tell your teacher, parent, or spouse that you struggle in an area and would be grateful if they would bring it to your attention any time they notice you doing that impulsive thing.

I know that it may sound like being impulsive is a bum deal. Let there be no mistake, it is a very difficult thing to get a handle on, but there are also some surprising advantages to being impulsive. For example, when you're working on a project and a better idea comes to mind, there's no time wasted in switching gears. If you ever become a performer on stage, being impulsive is called improv, and people pay to watch it!

12

The A-Team had Mr. T and I had Ms. T!

the Scoop

- ADDers are a warm-hearted group of people
- Most ADDers have a great sense of humor
- Having ADD or a Learning Disability does NOT mean that you are stupid!

It takes 3,000 cows to supply the NFL with enough leather for a year's supply of footballs.

The day high school started, I was anxious. Entering a new and much larger school was intimidating, and I was insecure about my every move.

One thing was certain, it was going to take a special teacher to deal with my special situation. Ms. Thielberg, whom everyone called Ms. T, was just what the doctor ordered. That first day in her Special Ed classroom, the name of which had been changed to the Study Skills classroom, seemed like all the others. We did the whole introduction thing, the rule thing, and then the goal thing. At the end of the class, she passed around a contract for all of us to sign. The contract stated all the rules such as: Follow directions, be in your seat before the bell, be prepared to learn, and keep your hands and feet to yourself. (Bob would have had a hard time with that one!)

The contract also stated that Ms. T would commit to giving us her very best. Under the statement, she signed her name. In turn, the contract had a place for us to sign. It stated that I, the student, would commit to give my very best. Each of us had to take the contract home to think about the kind of year we wanted to have before we signed it. Then, there was even a place on the paper for our parents to sign. That portion stated that they would commit to helping our educational process in any way they could.

She explained that spoken words are easily forgotten, but that a written contract would remain as a reminder in case either we, or she, went astray in our commitment.

I can remember thinking to myself, "This is her way of tricking us into doing more homework." But the more I thought about it, the more the idea inspired me. I'd never signed a contract before. It made the class seem more grown up and therefore more appealing. I signed!

There was something special about Ms. T. I couldn't put my finger on back then, but with hindsight, it was apparent that she had a gift for working with Special Ed kids.

ADDers are a warmhearted group of people and most of them have a good sense of humor. When you learn to tie these traits with procrastination, you often end up with a smooth-talking kid who knows how to get out of doing work. (Sorry ADDers, I am going to let everyone in on our secret.) We don't like to accept that the work is for our own good. We ADDers are masters at making excuses. We are masters at selling our point of view. I have read on many occasions that ADDers make great sales people. However, they struggle with the paper work that comes after the sale.

One of the things I loved about Ms. T was the fact that

she didn't let anyone smooth-talk her out of doing the work. She was skillfully able to combine good humor and discipline, cracking the whip on us on the one hand, yet allowing us moments of chaos and slapstick.

During the year I spent in Ms. T's class, I discovered more strategies for learning than ever before. Her creative approach gave each kid in her class the opportunity to develop and grow to a whole new level.

One of the first issues Ms. T addressed in class was the fact that most Special Ed students grow up with a couple of big misconceptions about themselves. I shared about this several chapters back; all Special Ed students, whether they have LD, ADD, ADHD, or LMNOP, at some point believe that they are stupid.

> **...It was apparent that she had a gift for working with Special Ed kids...**

This kind of mind-set is extremely counter-productive. Ms. T knew this and wanted to address it up front. She knew that our fear of revealing our "stupidity" could make it difficult for us to ask questions when something she was teaching wasn't making sense. That first day, she pronounced in a no-nonsense kind of voice, "There is no such thing as a stupid question in my class!" (She was so right! The truth is that the only stupid questions are the ones left unasked.) Unfortunately, we all had a hard time believing that she meant what she said. Eventually, though Ms. T drove into our brains was that everyone has moments when they just don't get it. She repeatedly told us that a person didn't have to be LD, ADD, ADHD, or LMNOP to not understand something. Too often, ADDers believe that these "things are only happening to me because I have ADD."

In reality, these "things" happen to everyone. Everyone has questions, and everyone has struggles, and if we write them off as the result of some disorder, then questions and struggles get unanswered.

From that day on, my hand was up more than it was down. I had questions that needed to be answered. The only one she couldn't answer was, "Why do men have nipples?"

One day, I was sitting at my desk struggling to read a book. It seemed like whenever I got done reading a page, I'd have no idea what I'd just read. Has this ever happened to you? This happened to me all the time. I ended up having to read something seven or eight times before it made sense. Do you think I enjoyed reading back then? NO WAY! It was so much work that it was barely worth the effort.

When I read something, I wanted to be able to read it once and understand it right then and there. After trying to read and understand the same paragraph for ten minutes, I got up, walked up to the trash can, and dumped all of my books. Ms. T laughed a little and asked what I was doing. I explained to her that reading wasn't worth my time when I had to read it ten times to make any sense of it. Her response was, "Read out loud." Wow! What a difference that made.

Because my brain is always in hyperdrive, there are too

> ...she didn't let anyone smooth-talk her out of doing the work...

many things in my head competing for my attention. It's not always going to be possible for me to sit and read a book while my brain is screaming, "Look at the butterfly outside the window. Go pet it!"

That's why I had to make reading more than just reading. When I first began to read out loud, I felt a little dorky and self-conscious. There was no denying it though, when I read out loud, I understood and remembered what I had just read ten times better than before. Not only was I seeing the letters, the words and the sentences, but I was hearing them too, and that made a world of difference.

Today, I love to read. I also love to look at my bookshelf filled with books I have actually read. It makes me want to give myself a big old pat on the back, and a scratch and sniff sticker.

I became a monster reader. I even started using a highlighter to mark the important portions of the book. Reading became more than reading; it was an activity.

The best place I have found to read out loud is on an airplane sitting in first class. I will get two pages into a book and, it never fails, someone always leans over and asks, "Would you please read to yourself?"

I smile at that person winningly and respond with, "No, I'm special, but if you would like, you could read it to me."

The biggest lesson Ms. T taught me that year is that I was capable of doing almost anything. It just may be that I would have to find a creative and unorthodox way to tackle challenging tasks.

Pep Talk Time

Keep thinking outside the box! This so-called disorder can be a great ride. I know it would be easier if there was one trick, one solution, or one answer, but when it comes to ADD there are more ways than any of us could ever imagine to combat the symptoms and make them work for us. The key is creativity! Utilize all the resources you can so that you have the best possible chance to make it. Don't be afraid to follow the advice of an unconventional teacher. It might be just the ticket! If you change things up every day, this ADD thing is going to be a great adventure. I don't know about you, but I'm looking forward to the ride. I just hope there are seat belts!

The Magic Notebook

the Scoop

- If you don't write it down, you'll forget about it
- ADDers come up with more ideas in a week than most people do in a year

Did you know that it takes four gallons of water for a cow to produce one gallon of milk?

Did you know that every sturgeon is born a male? When the sturgeon grows to a certain length it becomes a female. Guys, can you imagine if that happened to us? You go to bed one night and grow a few inches and you wake up the next morning and notice something's really different?

Have you ever-wondered why they put the word "natural" on bottled water? Isn't all water natural?

Did you know that a carp is a fish with lips?

If I give a cow one gallon of milk, can that cow produce four gallons of water? Can we then bottle that water and call it natural? (We would probably have to call it filtered.)

Each of the above questions was an "ADD moment" that I had some time in the past few months. Ordinarily, thinking about a fish with lips would entice me away from whatever else I'd be working on, but something I call my "Magic Notebook" has been keeping me on track for quite a few years now and has helped me manage a great deal of weird, potentially distracting thoughts.

Using a notebook to keep track of random thoughts and ideas was a technique Ms. T came up with to help us stay in the game. Ms. T knew it didn't take much to get us riled up and distracted from what we needed to be doing in class. Moreover, if one kid was being distracted by something, it was more than likely that he or she would suck other kids into the distraction.

There were times during class when someone would blurt out a crazy idea, someone else would build on it, and before you knew it, we had our own improv comedy show, complete with sets, costumes and audience participation. This would always end in someone peeing his or her pants from laughing too hard. Okay, I admit, there were days when we had fun in the Special Ed class. We would have loved to have every class be Comedy Central, but Ms. T kept us on a tight leash and made sure that we actually learned something.

When Ms. T made everyone in the class get a notebook, she told us that anytime we noticed something that could pull our attention away, we should write it down. The same went for any time we had an idea or thought that we wanted to spend more time on, or any time we noticed something funny. She explained to us that if we wrote all these things down and then closed the notebook, that the idea, thought, joke, or moment wouldn't be lost; it would be waiting for us right there on the page where we left it, to enjoy at a more appropriate time.

I don't know if a "Magic Notebook" will work for all

ADDers, but it helped me a great deal. I have stacks of notebooks to prove it still works for me today. Some of my best speaking and comedy ideas are penned in a notebook during times when I am trying to be focused on something else entirely. If you dig through a few of those notebooks, you will even find the place where I wrote down the idea for this book. All the material I shared at the beginning of this chapter has also been made into comedy material. The reason why I call it my Magic Notebook is because it helps me make the millions of ideas and thoughts that cross my mind into magic.

We would have loved to have every class be Comedy Central...

ADDers have more ideas than anyone I know. Unfortunately, the sad truth is that most of these ideas are lost because the mind can only remember so much.

I am sure you have experienced a moment when you had a great idea and the idea was so cool that you told yourself you would never forget it. Ten minutes later you were kicking yourself because your brilliant idea was gone, never to be recaptured. If only you'd written it down!

Using a notebook to write down whatever comes into your head is both a great way to capture and document how creative, smart and amazing you really are, AND to keep you on track with whatever else you're supposed to be doing when you have the idea.

Give the notebook a try and let me know if it works for you.

Pep Talk Time

You have more ideas pass through your brain than most people can imagine. These ideas are a double-edged sword. They can get you into trouble because they are always calling your name, begging you to give them attention so you don't forget them. The problem is timing. Have you noticed how some of your best ideas demand your attention at the worst possible time? Well, the best way to take care of this to be prepared! Go into any situation that will require your prolonged attention armed with your Magic Notebook and as soon as an idea pops into your head, write it down quickly and put the notebook away. Now you'll know that your idea will not escape and can be revisited at a better time. Mind you, the Magic Notebook is not an excuse to get distracted. Learn to use it as a tool and you'll be killing two birds with one stone; you'll have an easier time staying focused on the task at hand AND you'll build an incredible collection of million dollar ideas! A Magic Notebook can help you capture the gift of creativity and harness the wonderful ideas, thoughts, and moments that fill your mind every day.

Mild Distractions & "Hyperfocus"

13$\frac{1}{2}$

the Scoop

- A mild distraction can help you avoid falling into a major distraction
- Teachers don't like it when you click your clicker pens during class

On occasion, a notebook is not enough. Some days, my brain wants to play no matter what tools I have to help me stay on task. I want to play, my impulsivity is running at an all-time high, I've just eaten enough Little Debbie Snack Cakes to kill a horse, so I will begin scanning the room seeking a worthy distraction to sweep me up into an ADD moment.

Back in school, I would twist and turn in my seat, bounce my legs, play with a clicker pen and be very restless as I tried to concentrate on what was being taught. All these "ticks," as I discovered later in life, were actually coping mechanisms that I now call "mild distractions." These helped a part of my brain to stay occupied while the other part of my brain attempted to get some work done.

You may already be familiar with some of these mild distractions. They include playing with a Koosh ball or water ball, doing origami, or doodling. For some ADDers, a mild distraction is all they need to stay in the game. A mild distraction can go a long way to keep an ADDer focused; in fact, most ADDers who are unaware of what mild distractions are, discover a few on their own without really trying. How many of you ADDers out there find it much easier to do your work with the radio on?

When I was growing up, I can recall times when I tried doing the homework with my radio on. Of course, I had my music loud enough to shake the house! Mom would always come up to my room and ask, "How can you study with all this noise? I can't even hear myself think! Turn it down!" I always loved it when she would say things like, "I can't hear myself think!" My Mom used to say this a lot around me which to be honest used to freak me out a little. Why should she hear herself think? I didn't hear myself think. Was my mom hearing voices and what were those voices saying? Maybe some of those lice got into my Mom's head and stirred things up a bit. Maybe my mom was Special. Without thinking before opening my mouth, I would say, "Hey. Mom, sounds like you need to be in my Special Ed class.. You're acting a little special lately."

One great teacher can make a world of difference

By the look on my Mom's face, I quickly realized that a kid shouldn't question his mother's mental status. It just doesn't sound good. Do you remember when I mentioned impulsiveness? Sometimes I think impulsiveness should be called, "Foot-In-Mouth Syndrome." That was not a smart thing to say to Mom. My Mom, in her anger, made me shut my radio off, march downstairs with my homework, and sit at the dining room table. She told me that I needed to study in peace and quiet.

She made me sit at that table for a full hour. The problem was that she failed to notice that there was a clock on the wall in that room... a ticking clock. Do you have any idea how loud a ticking clock can be if you take out all the other ambient noise from a room? LOUD! Okay, ADDers love the sparkly, ADDers can get sucked into focusing on the ugly, and ADDers will always be distracted by the things that irritate them, like weird, out-of-place noises, smells, things, or people. For me, a ticking clock drives me nuts, and so for an hour I sat at that table, but didn't do any homework. I just sat there distracted with ideas on how I could kill the clock and get away with it. When my Mom came back into the room, she asked, "What are you doing with the meat tenderizer and what in the world happened to the clock?"

"Sorry Mom. The clock's dead. Might want to think digital next time."

This episode was the result of not having an adequate mild distraction. I lacked the one thing that could have kept my mind in the game. Instead, my mind locked onto the clock.

Why can a ticking clock drive me up a wall? I have no idea. Maybe this is one of those questions for the doc, but whatever the reason, I know nothing will change the fact that ticking clocks hold a strange power over me. Sure, I could try and destroy all the ticking clocks in the world, but that's not even realistic for guys like Captain Hook. So the only option I have is to know what mild distraction works to drown out the major distraction of a clock.

For me, the radio is a great mild distraction. However, it may not be for you. As an ADDer, you need to find out what mild distractions work for you. Try the Kooshball, whip out the water ball, crank up the radio, or pull out a pocket notebook to doodle. Finding a few positive mild distractions that work for you will give you the freedom to know that wherever you are, despite any major distractions around you, you have the ability to do something to help yourself stay focused.

Since I have learned that something as small as a ticking clock can drive an ADDer nuts, I have tried to become more aware of the fact that some of my mild distractions can be major distractions for others.

I must admit, I learned the importance of this the hard way. Once upon a time, I was sitting in art class trying to figure out what my next project was going to be. As the class sat in silence, thinking, my mind began to drift from the task at hand, so I began to click the end of my clicker pen to keep my mind in the game. In the same way a clock can be loud in a silent room, a clicker pen can be just as loud. As I began to click the pen, the clicks were slow and somewhat spread apart, but two minutes into my clicking, I was clicking with the speed of light. I was clicking like I was hopped up on Pop Rocks and Fun Dip. Little did I know that with each click of my pen, my teacher was getting more and more angry. Every time I clicked my pen, it was as if I was jamming a needle into the cranium of my instructor.

For some of my instructors, this would not have been a bad thing, but I loved my art teacher, so when she finally snapped at me, I was a little taken aback. In front of the whole class she said, sounding quite aggravated, "BEN! ENOUGH WITH THE PEN!"

I was a little embarrassed, but nonetheless, I got the point. I stopped clicking. The room got silent again as everyone resumed their creative thinking.

Sadly though, it only took five minutes before I began

to slowly click my pen again. Before I got to full clicking speed, my teacher snapped again, "BEN!"

To a non-ADD-person, it may have looked like I was clicking on purpose just to irritate the teacher, but the truth is, I was clicking without really thinking about it. It was my brain's way of saying, "If you want me staying in the game, we are going to have to make this a little less boring."

The third time my teacher had to address my incessant clicking, I thought for sure she was going to beat me with a ruler, Scotch tape my hands together, gag me with an eraser, put me in a burlap bag, and drop me in the local DuPage River as catfish bait. Instead, she took away my clicker pen... and snapped it in half... and then snapped the halves in half.

> **A 'hyperfocused' individual will lose track of time, miss meals, or skip meetings.**

To this day, I try really hard to identify which of my mild distractions may be a major distraction for others. Those things that may be a major distraction for others, I save for times when I am alone. For all the others, I have them ready to use at any given moment.

You will find that the more you use your mild distractions, the more you will learn that not only can they work to help you focus, but they can also help you to unfocus. That's right! There are going to be times when an ADDer needs to unfocus because the brain is locked in "hyperfocus."

We all know what focus means, so you can only

imagine what "hyperfocus" means. My definition of "hyperfocus" is this: Any time one thing consumes a person so much that the person is unaware of anything else. A "hyperfocused" individual will lose track of time, miss meals, or skip meetings.

There are many ways an ADDer can fall into a "hyperfocused" state. You may be able to relate to a time when, for no reason whatsoever, a random idea popped into your mind. If the idea had nothing to do with what you were doing in that moment, and you didn't have ADD, you would have probably dismissed it and went on about your business

But it happened to you, so that popping idea didn't just take up a small portion of your mental computer screen, but took over the entire thing, like a bad virus. So what began as a simple passing thought became an all-consuming state that is known as the "hyperfocus."

One bad grade does not mean I'm stupid!

Let's pretend that you've studied really hard for a test and didn't get the grade you wanted. Your mind begins to race with negative thoughts about your poor performance and how it will affect the rest of your life and "boom," you're hyperfocused on the "problem" to the exclusion of everything else going on around you. How can you not be when what seems like one-hundred million thoughts come rushing into your mind?

With all of these thoughts gallivanting through your head in every which direction, it's hard to pinpoint the actual problem, and therefore impossible to find a solution. You may feel lost in a sea of ideas or fears with no idea how to get out.

This is where a nice, mild distraction comes to the rescue. It can help slow the brain down enough so that you can hop out of "hyperfocus," take a few deep breaths, and give yourself an opportunity to separate reality from fantasy.

When you're hyperfocused and stuck in a negative mind-set, this is what might be going through your mind:

"I can't believe how poorly I did on that test!! And I studied so hard. Well, this confirms it: I'm a total idiot. I'm going to flunk out of this class and then the school. No college will ever want me and no employer will hire me. I'm just the biggest loser on the planet and will be sweeping floors in McDonald's for the rest of my life. Why am I so stupid? It's just so unfair! And my parents are going to be so mad! I promised them that I would bring up my grades and now this! My life stinks! I can't tell anyone about this bad grade because they will probably laugh at me and not want to be friends anymore. I mean, who would want to be friends with a loser like me. I wouldn't!!"

Wow! All that because of one bad grade, on one test, in one subject, during one semester of school, in one year of your life?? Seems like you'd be overreacting just a bit.

Now if you took the time to slow down and really think things through, maybe this would be the conversation you'd have with yourself:

"What a bummer that I didn't score so well on that test. And I studied too. I wonder if I just didn't read the right chapters? I'm gonna meet with the teacher to ask her to explain some of these answers that I missed. I should find out how the other students did on this test; maybe I'm not the only one who found it difficult. Anyway, it's just one test. There will be others and I'll be sure to get extra help in this subject so I can do better next time. And even if I don't do so well in this subject, there's algebra and art that I'm really great at. I can't be great at everything; no one can. Now I'm going to put this one behind me and focus on the next class. I know everything will work out. One bad grade does not mean I'm stupid!"

Use whatever means necessary to fight the human tendency to focus on the negative. So much of your future success depends on how you respond to the various things that happen to you as you go through life. I'll be honest with you and tell you that it takes years to learn to catch yourself going into a negative tailspin and to reverse the cycle, but it's well worth the effort. A mild distraction is just one tool to help distract you before you get completely sucked into a downward spiral. Use it!

Pep Talk Time

There are many tools available to you to help you combat some of the more negative aspects of ADD. I believe that "mild" distractions can play a huge role in helping you be more productive and less likely to hyperfocus on the wrong things. Take the time to figure out what helps you stay in the game without driving the other people in the room mad with annoyance. And be sure to explain to the people around you what you are doing. They may think that you're just messing with a toy, but it's so much more than that. Getting them to understand will create another layer of support for you to become a more effective student, employee, parent or spouse.

13³⁄₈

Run, Ben! Run!

the Scoop

- Exercise can help ADDers focus

It's possible to lead a cow upstairs...but not downstairs.

Five years ago I was in a crowd of thirty-five thousand people. We were all waiting for the same thing: the sound of a gun! When the sound of the shot reverberated through the cool, morning air, we all began to move one step closer to the finish line.

The Indianapolis Mini Marathon is the largest Mini Marathon in the world, and to be honest, I had no idea how I found myself standing next to some of the best trained athletes I had ever seen.

It all started about nine months before the race. I had read somewhere that exercising could help ADDers focus. Since I was trying to learn as much as I could about being ADD, I decided to give it a try.

At first, I started running on a treadmill. Well, I don't know if you could call it running as much as fast walking. For the first month and a half, I didn't notice much difference mentally, other than the fact my body was telling me to stop.

However, like with most tasks that are a little difficult, there's a hump that needs to be gotten over before you start to reap the rewards. When I got over that hump, BAM! I saw a big difference. I could stay focused on one thing longer, organize my thoughts, prioritize my day, and then see tasks to completion. On the days I ran, I did my best work. On the days I chose not to run, I struggled.

Exercise gets the "skippies" to come out and play!

Exercise gets the "skippies" to come out and play! Before a test, ADDers should run a mile. Before homework, ADDers should go play kick the can. Before making that big decision, ADDers need to go swim a few laps. Exercising has helped me almost as much as any medication I have ever taken. Some of my best mental work occurs while I am running.

I was speaking at a church recently when I received an interesting question on the topic of quieting my mind. A student asked me, "Ben how do you have a quiet time with God if your ADD brain never quits?"

A quiet time is something Christians do when they want to spend time with God. It's a time when everything external is turned off and tuned out so that an open mind and heart is receptive to the voice of God. Most quiet times are spent reading the Bible, or doing a devotional - stuff that most ADDers dread doing.

I answered the question, "I spend my quiet times running."

This was a quiet time that they had never heard of, and so I had to explain. When I run, my mind slows down. I can turn off the world and focus. I can pray and meditate without distractions. Most quiet times for me consist of running a mile. If I end up running five miles, then you know I had a lot to pray about that day.

If you were to look at me, you would notice I am not your typical runner. In fact, I run like a turtle. But hanging in my office are five medals from five mini-marathons. I'm not necessarily a huge fan of running, but I love what it does for me mentally, and of course it's nice to reap the health benefits as well.

Pep Talk Time

Sometimes what everyone calls "being hyper" is just an ADDer's body wanting to blow off some steam. We were not designed to sit for long periods of time - too bad schools haven't come up with a way to teach us while we are simultaneously engaged in some physical activity! (Picture a class of ADD students spinning and at the same time watching an educational program about history...hmmm.) We need to be moving with a capital M. Don't hesitate to go run a lap. Go ahead and get a can to kick around or go play ball or take some martial arts classes. It just might be the addition of regular, heart-pounding exercise that will help you have an easier time sitting down to get some work done. If you're really ambitious, I suggest trying a game of dodgeball... by yourself. Let me know how it goes.

14

Box o' Rewards

- Learn the answer to the question "What motivates me?"
- ADDers struggle with delaying gratification. That means dessert is usually eaten first!
- ADDers love rewards

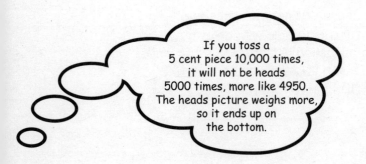

What motivates an ADDer more than anything? Just one word of praise... or a reward or prize... or even frosting-- any one of these will get us going.

We love instant gratification which sometimes can be a pitfall. I was never motivated when a teacher would tell us at the beginning of the year that if we accomplished this or that, then, at the end of the year, there would be a great reward. It might have motivated some of the kids, but not me. If I was going to work on something, it had to offer a quick payoff. (I have heard that this is one of the reasons many ADDers struggle with addictions. Addictive substances offer quick payoffs.)

Thankfully, Ms. T had developed an incredible reward system that kept me and the rest of our class motivated all year long. Ms. T understood that if she was going to keep us moving forward, she would have to come up with creative ways to reward us. She had a box she called, "Box o' Rewards" Inside this box were coupons for free stuff, and also movie passes, CD's, and the key to a brand new car. (Just kidding about the car!) Any time we did something that was noteworthy, a ticket with our name on it would go into a second box. At the end of the week, she would pick out a few tickets, and if your name was on one of them, it would be "magic box" diving time.

Every kid wanted to have the most tickets in the drawing; the competition was fierce. The more tickets, the better your chance of winning.

I responded to the reward system very well. Being able to see the prizes and knowing that the prizes could be attained in a short amount of time kept me motivated.

For many people, the things they are working for would be considered long-term goals. Their hard work comes from the vision of what the future may hold. Keeping that goal in sight helps maintain the motivation to see the journey through.

For example, a freshman in college may have a goal to graduate in four years with honors so that they can have a shot at getting hired for the most prestigious, highest paying jobs out there. For four years, that student finds motivation and discipline from the reward that is yet to come. When the student reaches his goal, it is because he never took his eyes off of the reward. This long-term sacrifice is called delayed gratification.

I was never good with waiting for my rewards, so Mrs. T's magic box was an ideal solution to the problem.

As I said, most ADDers want what they want NOW. If you go back to the chapter where I talked about being impulsive, you will quickly understand that mixing instant gratification and impulsivity together is as dangerous as crossing the streams from two proton packs. (See *Ghostbusters* for more on that subject.)

What I have learned about myself is that I will always struggle with long-term goals/rewards. The worst question someone can ask me is, "Where do you see yourself in five years?"

I have no idea! I can only tell you where I am going to be in the next week.

Not being able to have a clear vision for my future can make long-term planning very difficult if not impossible without some outside help. Not to worry! Here again I apply the principle of "baby steps". I start by planning for the next day. When I learn how to do that, I plan two days out, and so on and so forth. Realistically it may take years to learn how to plan a week ahead, but it's well worth the effort-- I will get a lot more done if I master this basic skill of organization.

> **The worst question someone can ask me is, "Where do you see yourself in five years?"**

I used to write out my long-term goals, just like all the motivational/goal-setting books tell a person to do, but I knew deep down inside that the list would fail to keep me motivated and on track. In fact, those "goal lists" would make me feel like a total loser because invariably when I would look at them months down the road, I'd see that I had achieved very few of the goals that I had set for myself.

But my lack of accomplishment wasn't just an issue of long-term goal setting vs. instant gratification. What I discovered was that with my highly creative and hyperactive mind, I would think of far too many things I wanted to accomplish. Instead of having one or two practical, obtainable goals, I had fifty incredibly lofty and difficult to achieve goals that would take not days or weeks, but months and years to achieve.

A few years ago, my wife and I sat down and wrote out our individual goals for the year. My list was very long as usual. I guess I was hoping that if I just put enough goals on the list, I would be bound to reach one of them.

The following year, my wife found the list under a pile of papers and coffee cups while we were cleaning out my office. Of course, I had forgotten all about it. As she read down the list, I became more and more discouraged because not one goal could receive a checkmark of completion. I hadn't achieved a single thing. I felt like a big old loser!

For two days, I sulked about my lack of achievement. A whole year had gone by and I hadn't done a darn thing! My wife snapped me out of my funk with a swift kick to the head (figuratively speaking) and said, "Don't just sit there! Do something about it!"

I remembered hearing a speaker say that you can always spot success by the size of a person's day timer. (He was wrong.) So, of course, I ran to my local office supplies store and bought a big, very expensive day planner, and two days later, I promptly lost it. I spent a couple of years going through calendars and planners like they were socks, but that whole system never worked for me.

I, like most people with learning difficulties, have tried everything known to man to stay organized and motivated, and to work towards long-term goals: day planners, wall calendars, handheld gizmos, cork boards with lots of push-pins, jumbo dry erase boards, a multitude of different kinds of to-do lists, motivational books, tapes and CD's, and still, nothing seemed to work. Most of these tools appeared to have about a one-month shelf life before I would lose focus and fall back into my chaotic, spur-of-the-moment ways. So where did that leave me?

In my search for the perfect goal-obtaining system, I discovered that there is no one system that will always work for me. All along, I was being sucked into believing that there was only one way to reach my goals, and that way would be found in the laws and principles given by some famous motivational speaker. Then, finally, I realized that the only true system that can work for me is the system of self-awareness.

ADDers need a reward system to keep going.

As individuals, we all have our struggles and issues. Sure, we can generalize about personalities, "he's such a comedian" or "she's so driven," but in the end, each person is an individual who needs a customized system to reach his or her goals. As I became more aware of what worked for me and what didn't, I had to accept that I would never be someone who carries a day planner and that I still could be successful!

I also realized that I needed to go over my huge "to-do" list with my highly organized and realistic wife at least once a week. ADDers are not great at judging how long any one task may take them and usually overestimate their resources and abilities in relation to what needs to be done. I love to pile all kinds of projects and tasks on my "to-do" list. As a result, I tend to be a master of unfinished projects. I start one project on my list and then notice another, so I leave the first project and start on the second, and so on and so forth, until I'm juggling about ten different things and wondering why I'm so stressed out.

ADDers are not great at judging how long any one task may take them...

Although a little humbling at first, I found it helpful to have another person go through my list with me and ask me some very hard questions about my priorities. At first, my ego didn't like the idea that I couldn't "do it all," but when I noticed how much more I was getting done and that I was actually bringing projects to completion, I knew that I had discovered another piece of a jigsaw puzzle that was helping me make the best of my ADD traits.

One of the nicest things about bringing projects to completion has, of course, been the opportunity to reward myself for a job well done.

Since receiving frequent rewards is a highly stimulating incentive for an ADDer, I now know to break up any large goals I have into smaller goals that can be achieved more quickly, thus resulting in more frequent rewards. Pretty smart of me, eh?

◇◇◇◇◇◇◇◇◇◇◇◇◇◇◇◇◇◇◇◇◇

Ultimately, the best system for getting organized and achieving any goals, big or small, is self-awareness. Study yourself, so you can learn and identify what inspires you, what motivates you, what challenges you, what drives you nuts, what depresses you, what causes you to fail, and what helps you to succeed. Like it or not, having and achieving long-term goals is a huge part of living a fulfilling and meaningful life, but there is more than one way to get there. Jim Rohn, one of the world's most renowned business philosophers says it best, "You will never be able to change the fact that summer will always come after spring, that winter will always come after fall. You will never be able to change the fact that night will always come after day and that day will always come after night. As much as you try, you will never be able to squeeze one more hour out of a twenty-four hour day. There are many things you can not change, but one thing you can change is yourself."

The only way we can begin to make positive changes in our lives is by becoming more self-aware. Every person should have control and ownership of his or her own life if he or she wants to live it with meaning and to reach his or her full potential.

As I have made a conscious effort to learn more about ADD and what it means in my life, I have become more aware of my strengths and weaknesses. I have learned that in some cases, changing myself is simply changing my approach. I know I am not good at planning for my future so I found someone who would be good to help me with this. I am not good at saving my money for tomorrow, so I found someone who was good at saving to help me. I am not the best at keeping a schedule, so I found an assistant who was.

In some cases, changing is simply asking for help. A

change for you may be finding a financial planner, a coach, teacher, parent, or an accountability partner.

Ms. T was my teacher for a year, and that year, I changed.

Ms. T transferred to a new school the following year. All the teachers who followed her built upon what Ms. T started, but it was during the one year when Ms. T was my teacher that everything began to fall into place.

The right teacher or mentor can make quite an impact on you in just one year. For a low self-esteem kid like me, there was nothing better than experiencing someone like Ms. T who knew how to treat a student like a star. She made me feel like less of "a mistake," because she treated me like I was "on purpose!"

Ms. T saw right through me, and as I look back to that first year of high school, I realize that it may have been the first year I actually learned how to learn.

On top of that, I learned to value learning. She treated me like a star because when she looked at me, she saw a star.

I don't know if she would remember this, but every so often, when I would walk into her class, she would say, "Here's Ben Glenn!" in her best announcer voice and explain how she felt that my name, one day, would be announced in front of thousands.

Man, did that ever make me feel cool! Oddly enough, my career allows me to have a chance to speak in front of thousands of people. Sometimes, before I step out on stage, I can hear her voice saying, "Here's Ben Glenn!"

Pep Talk Time

*I'm keeping this short because I promised myself
that as soon as I get done with this chapter I could
go fishing, and I have to hurry because my bait is
going off and stinking up the place. I wonder, do fish
like dead worms? I need to learn to type faster!
What motivates you, what gets you excited, what
is a "reward" that you're willing to work for? Will
you read a chapter in your textbook if you know
immediately afterwards you can go outside and play
basketball? Would you finish off those last four math
problems if you had a Little Debbie Snack Cake waiting
for you? Would you take care of your chores if you
knew you could watch your favorite TV show?
It's okay that we need a little instant gratification in our
lives to keep us motivated. Sometimes it's going to be up
to you to set the rewards to help motivate yourself. Mom
and Dad will not always remember to have that treat
waiting for you when you are done with your work, so
learn to treat yourself, but make sure you keep it honest.
Treating yourself without doing the work first is no treat
at all; it's just laziness. Work hard for the payoff, and over
time the payoff will be greater than you can imagine.*

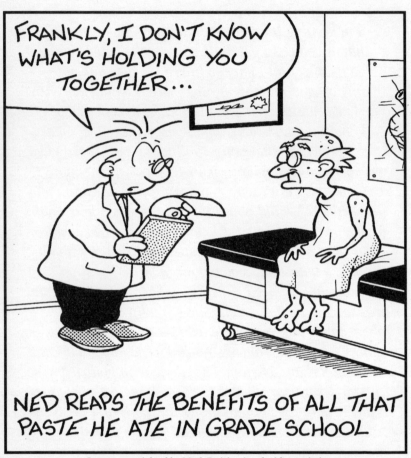

15
No More
Mr. Benchwarmer

the Scoop

- Seek counsel from people you trust
- Come out from behind the walls of self-doubt
- ADDers have great potential just waiting to burst out

In Cleveland, Ohio it is illegal to catch mice without a hunting license.

My basketball career started in the seventh grade. I wasn't the best player on the team; in fact, I was a bench warmer.

So after I made the team in the seventh grade, I kept trying out each year, and kept making teams. I thought that the coaches looked at me and saw that I was big, and figured that meant I must be able to play basketball.

When they actually saw me play outside of tryouts, though, they would put me back on the bench. I had no problem with that. There was something about having to perform in front of a crowd that scared me to death anyway. On the bench, I was safe. I'd never let anyone down or be made fun of for missing a shot. (Plus, if you think about it, the bench is the best seat in the house. No one ever sits in front of you, and it's the closest seat to the concession stand.)

Entering ninth grade, I was looking forward to another

year as a bench warmer. But Coach Stevens had different plans for me.

Coach Stevens was a young, right-out-of-college teacher who still drove the same car he had in high school: a rusty, old, faded red Chevy Nova that needed a muffler.

Though his car was wearing out, he had great dreams of moving forward. He was a teacher in the elementary school, and started his coaching career as the ninth-grade basketball coach. Since I was a ninth grader who theoretically played basketball, we were destined to cross paths, and I am thankful that we did. That first day of practice with the new coach was quite memorable.

You see, Coach Stevens went to school in Platville, Wisconsin, where he had just completed a basketball program that was all about conditioning. When a coach uses the words, "Get on the line," the first day of practice, you know you're in trouble.

"Get on the line," in basketball lingo, means that you will soon be very sweaty and out of breath. And I was. Oh, how I hated to run! Thoughts of quitting crossed my mind as my lungs burned and sharp, stabbing pains in my side made me wonder if I was having a heart attack. In the history of first-day basketball practices, I think Coach Stevens could win the award for getting more kids to lose their lunch than any other coach.

Although I contemplated quitting those first few practice sessions, I ended up hanging in there. I think it might have been because the coach did all the running with us. I had never heard of a coach working out side-by-side with his players. It's easy, as a player, to believe that a coach is just running you into the ground for his own personal fun, but Coach wasn't asking us to do anything he wasn't willing to do himself. And because of his willingness to lead us in what was the most unpleasant part of practice, Coach soon had the team's grudging respect.

I still don't know if Coach ever knew about the baggage I brought to the locker room that year. You know-- the whole Special Ed thing... If he knew anything, he surely didn't let on, because I can tell you that he always looked at me as if I had great potential just waiting to burst out of me and onto the basketball court.

It kind of freaked me out a little to have a coach push me the way he did, seeing some type of potential in me even though I wasn't exactly what I would call a go-getter on the court. Maybe he saw what my older brother, Sam, was doing on the varsity team and hoped that athletic talent ran in the family. Whatever the case, when I stepped out onto that court, Coach expected great things from me.

> **I had great potential just waiting to burst out of me and onto the basketball court.**

During the first few weeks of practice, I have to believe Coach was greatly disappointed in me. I ran through practice the way I was running through life. I was mostly just going through the motions. There was no passion, no drive and very little work ethic.

This was just another result of my many years of feeling like a mistake. Ms. T. aside, no one really expected much out of me, and though I may have had great potential, people weren't exactly lining up to tap into it.

Even though academically I was managing to hold my own (more or less), in general I had learnt to expect the bare minimum out of life, so I gave life the bare minimum back. Not many challenged me to excel because I was the special kid. Hardly anyone pushed me to try harder because I was the special kid.

And if I complained enough, cried enough, and didn't do enough, well, it was because I was the special kid. By the time I entered the ninth grade, I was an expert bench-warmer in more ways than one.

What I didn't realize is that every time I used the "I'm the special kid" excuse to avoid facing life, I got a little weaker. A great word to describe my

> **I knew he saw someone who was more than just a Special Ed kid with little to offer.**

attitude in life at that point was "atrophy." Atrophy is the weakening of a muscle from the lack of use. Up until that point, I had learned to just get by, but I was in for a great awakening.

After a few weeks of practice, I saw myself destined to be back on the bench where I had spent much of the last two years. When game day rolled around, I was excited. I might be warming the bench, but at least I had a new uniform to do it in! It was great to have left those nasty, old junior high uniforms behind. They had been way too tight and liked to ride up into places where things should never ride up.

I sauntered into the locker room, feeling all cool, ready for the usual pep-talk that Coach would give us before each game. I was a little early, so I decided that I still had time for a snack. I sat down by my locker, peeled back some of the wrapping from the Snickers bar I was able to snag from the concession stand, took a bite, and looked up to see the names of the players who would be starting the game, spelled out in crisp whiteness on the chalkboard. And…there was MY name!! The piece of Snickers bar that I had bitten off got lodged in my throat and I started choking and gagging as Coach entered the locker room and began to go over our plays.

After performing a Heimlich on myself and coughing up a bunch of nougat and melted chocolate mixed in with some caramel on one of my teammates, I tried to figure out what jerk was playing a practical joke on me. I stole stealthy glances at the guys on my team, but they were all focused on Coach and what he was saying. No one was acting suspicious or even looking in my direction. Could it be?

Reality began setting in. Coach was really expecting me to start. No bench for "the special kid" at this game. I didn't know what to do. I wasn't prepared. This had do be a mistake!

But no, no mistake. Coach started talking about the guy I was to be guarding. I nodded like I understood what he wanted me to do, but inside I was questioning his judgment. Surely there had to be someone better prepared than me to play, but I knew better than to question the coach. (I remember one kid who did that once in the eighth grade. I think he's still running laps.)

As the team left the locker-room, I sat glued to my seat in shock. Coach walked over to me, put a hand on my shoulder and said, "Give me everything you've got! Don't leave anything out on that court!"

I had yet to give anything "all I had." This was mostly because I felt like I didn't have much to give. When Coach looked at me, however, I knew he saw someone who was more than just a Special Ed kid with little to offer. That night, he gave me a chance to go out onto that court as a starter, and prove to myself that I was better than just a bench warmer.

The game went by in a flash. Did I play flawlessly? No, but I learned that being in the game was FAR better than sitting on that bench.

The fact that someone saw a starter rather than a bench warmer in me inspired me. Someone saw beyond the walls I had built around my life. Someone saw past the mask I put on for protection. Someone actually believed that I had what it took to do great things, even when I didn't believe it myself.

In the book <u>Wild at Heart</u>, John Eldredge says, "It's not a question-- it's the question, the one every boy and man is longing to ask: Do I have what it takes?"

"Do I have what it takes?"

"Do I have what it takes?"

When I read this book a couple of years back, I actually got chills. This is the question I have been asking myself all these years. I didn't know it, but as soon as I read this passage in the book, a light went on. (I love how books can help verbalize feelings and thoughts that I never can-- this is one big reason why I continue reading even when it still doesn't come naturally.)

Finally, I was able to pinpoint one of the greatest desires of my life. I wanted the answer to the question, "Do I have what it takes?"

In the ninth grade, Coach Stevens got me on the road to answering that question when he put my name alongside the other starting players on that chalkboard. Though it took many years before I could answer, "Yes, I have what it takes!" with passion and confidence, that day, Coach Stevens got that ball rolling. When someone believes in you, their faith has a tendency to rub off on you.

For the rest of that season, the team worked on basketball, while I worked on life. As soon as I got a taste of the fact that I just might have potential, I began to feel like I was becoming the young man I was always meant to be.

When we go through a hard time in our lives, it is easy to become blinded by our circumstances and hardships to the exclusion of everything else. It's hard to be motivated when you can't see a hopeful, bright future. One way to overcome this challenge is to seek out positive individuals who speak encouragement and hope into your life. And when you find them, hang onto their every word-- they are not just telling you a pretty story-- they really do see something in you that you are not yet able to see in yourself.

When someone believes in you, their faith has a tendency to rub off on you.

In the movie *Hook*, Peter Panning, an overweight workaholic, is stuck in Neverland trying to rescue his children. The Lost Boys are convinced that Peter Panning is the one and only Peter Pan. The problem is that Peter Panning has forgotten the fact that he's Peter Pan. In order to help him remember his roots, the Lost Boys put him through a day of Peter Pan training. He fails miserably. At the end of the day, everyone is hungry, especially Peter. Dishes and pans cover every inch of the table, but instead of being filled to the brim with food, they are empty. Well, at least they look empty to Peter; to the Lost Boys, they have never seemed more full. Peter sits and watches as the Lost Boys appear to be mimicking eating, but all of a sudden, Peter is caught up in their enthusiasm, his eyes are opened, and what he couldn't see moments ago is now a glorious feast before his very eyes. He joins in the gluttony and probably has the best meal of his life.

For so many years, I was blinded to my potential like Peter Panning, but when I allowed myself to be caught up in someone else's enthusiasm for what I had to offer, my life began to change. The glimpse of the potential others saw in me helped me to transform my attitude. It took time, but little by little, with support and encouragement from some key individuals, I actually started believing in myself.

Hopefully, you will have the fortune of finding a Ms. T, or a Coach Stephens, or the Lost Boys, or a compassionate parent, to help you to come out from behind the walls of self-doubt and to shine in all of your ADD glory.

But if you do not have a mentor, or a guide, don't lose heart. Remember that no matter how little talent you feel you have, no matter how far in the dungeon you are placed, no matter how alone you feel, you ARE filled with potential. I promise you that even if no one has believed in you yet, you are more than your "special" label. You are valuable.

Begin to let your creative and authentic self out in

positive and productive ways. Seek counsel from people you trust, and ask them to help you develop your talents. Let any small piece of praise sink in, so that you have fuel to keep you going. Gradually, your efforts will snowball, and people will notice. More importantly, you will begin to believe in your own ability to overcome, and with that belief, you can do anything!

Pep Talk Time

The protective walls you have built in your life can be a blessing and a curse. Nothing gets in or out. You may have minimized the pain of being teased and put down, but you're also not allowing the real you to blossom. All those gifts and talents you have are hiding behind your wall. If you're fortunate, someone with experience and a passion for helping you reach your full potential will come along, see beyond your walls, and work really hard to break them down so that you can come out of your self-imposed jail and make the most of life. You can wait for that to happen, but then why wait? Begin to take steps to recognize your own potential. Don't be afraid! You've been through so much already, and whether you know it yet or not, you do have what it takes. I believe in you!

Conclusion

God Makes No Junk

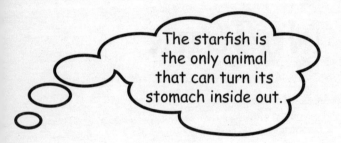

Based on the response I get from parents, teachers and students when they hear me proclaim that I love being ADD, there is no question that on some level people who work closely with ADDers or who have ADD themselves, know that ADD is not the curse that many people seem to think it is. Personally, I can't imagine being normal. How utterly boring that would be!

About ten years ago, I was speaking to a group of middle-school students. When I had finished telling my story of being labeled a special kid, I opened up the session for questions. One of the students asked me "If you could go back in time, would you change the fact that you were a special kid?"

I thought about that question for a moment and the story of my life rushed through my mind: the day I was labeled, the parade of tiny classrooms, the BD kid, the horrible bus rides, the first time I learned to write my name, the day the old Chinese doctor told me I had gas, the teacher who didn't give up on me, the coach who saw potential in me, and memory after memory, good and bad, flooded in. I looked out at that crowd of young, fresh faces and told them what I have told every crowd since then: "I wouldn't change a thing!"

In the spring of 2003, I was the keynote speaker at a banquet for the Fellowship of Christian Athletes. The message I gave was called "God Makes No Junk!" In it, I shared my story of being labeled and how God used the people around me to give me the chance to make something of myself. I shared my struggles that you have read about, and also the victories I have had, and then concluded my talk the way I conclude all my talks: I drew.

> **I would not swap my ADD brain for a normal one no matter how much money they offered me.**

As dramatic, beautiful music thunders, I use chalk to whip out a drawing of a brightly-colored landscape. I cover a canvas that measures about eight by six feet, in about twelve minutes. This isn't like Pictionary or sidewalk chalking. This is a theatrical explosion of color and sound, and every time I perform, my ADD has a great time.

You want to know something? I would have never become a performing artist and speaker had it not been for my ADD. And this is one of the many reasons why I would not swap my ADD brain for a normal one no matter how much money they offered me. (Who are "they?" I don't know; it just sounded good!)

When I finished my drawing at that FCA banquet, the emcee got up to say a closing prayer. He said, "Tonight, God has given me hope. For years I have prayed that my son would grow out of his ADD. I prayed that somehow he would wake up one morning and the ADD would be gone. I've always wanted my son to be normal because I see him struggle so much every day, and it breaks a father's heart. And tonight my prayers have finally been answered, just not in the way I thought they would be. Tonight I realized that ADD can be a blessing, and with God's help, He will lead me to teach my son that 'God Makes No Junk!' My son is special."

I had a chance to meet this man and his son after the program and it was great to know that from that day forward he was going to look at his kid in a totally different light and what a tremendous difference this change in a father's attitude would make in a son's life.

The opportunity that I have to inspire others through my story and art is another reason why I would never give up being ADD.

The final reason that I am thankful for my ADD is less straight-forward, but no less important. The Bible says in the book of James, "Consider it pure joy, my friends, any time you face trials, because you know the testing of your faith will develop perseverance."

Whether you read the Bible or not, there is no debating the wisdom found in this verse. Every bump and bruise I felt along my unconventional journey served a purpose. They gave me a chance to grow. They gave me a chance to overcome, and to persevere. They helped me discover who I was. They helped me find ways to live more effectively. They gave me the confidence to know that I could get through any obstacle.

So you see, learning to love your ADD and your ADD traits is not such a strange thing after all; part of your life's journey is about accepting, understanding and making ADD work for you so that one day you wake up and realize that if the ADD characteristics were to be taken from you, you'd be giving up some of your best features.

I hope that some of what I have shared has helped you see that ADD is not something that you need to fear, deny or flee. An ADDer's path may not be an easy one, but persistence and perseverance will pay off for you in many great and unimaginable ways and I suspect that you too will be able to say that you "wouldn't change a thing."

Pep Talk Time

You did it! You finished the book!
This is just like Jimmy hitting the last shot in the movie 'Hoosiers', or Rocky knocking out that big Russian in the movie 'Rocky IV', or Happy Gilmore sinking that last putt, or Tin Cup hitting that hole in one, or the Titans winning that last game, or that clown fish which found, 'Nemo'. YOU DID IT! Crank up the tunes, rip open a box of Little Debbies, it's celebration time! Hey it's not every day that an ADDer finishes reading a book. So you should be proud of yourself. You came, you saw, and you read this book! You da MAN! (Or WOMAN!)
Now take what you have learned and run with it. Use this book as momentum to find joy in being ADD and being on a quest of how you can turn ADD from a challenge to a blessing. Don't allow any label to hold you back from becoming a better you. You have what it takes, now go and live it out. Take the gift of ADD and go and hit that last shot, knock the cover off the ball, sink that putt, win that race, and knock one out of the park. Learn to be free from the label; Learn to be free to be you. Enjoy!

Bonus!

Ben's Top Ten List for Parents

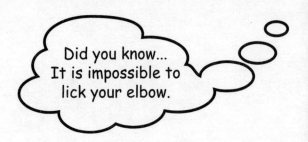

When your child is diagnosed and labeled with any kind of disorder, this can be just as hard on the parent as it is on the child. Having recently become a parent myself, I know first-hand that there are few things as frustrating, scary and unwelcome as the news that something is wrong with my kid. My oldest daughter's first ear infection was a complete tragedy for me. She was cranky and refused to eat or sleep and I was having a nervous breakdown. Then the doctor prescribed antibiotics and seven days later, my beautiful girl was covered in horrible, red hives from the top of her head to her small feet. The itching was so severe that she could not sleep for two nights straight. There was screaming and crying, mostly mine. My wife had to slap me upside the head and tell me to "snap out of it".

What I'm getting at is that it was hard for me to remain cool, calm and collected in a situation where I had no clue how to make things better for my little girl. The feeling of helplessness was overwhelming and in no small part because I'm no expert on childhood diseases and really have very little knowledge about such things as ear infections, antibiotics, and hives. For all I knew, she could die from these things or be disabled for life! As usual, my mind jumped to the worst case scenario.

Now that I'm a parent, I really feel for my parents. They had it rough with me from the get go.

I decided to come into the world a full two months early and was stuck in an aquarium in the hospital for weeks hooked up to all kinds of tubes and wires. After getting released from the hospital, I continued to struggle with asthma for the first couple of years of my life.

Then, when I grew out of asthma and my parents could breathe a sigh of relief, they were in for another shock. (A shock that I sometimes wonder if they've yet recovered from.) I discovered the joys of digging into my diaper and wiping its contents, with great passion and creativity, on all accessible flat surfaces. And an artist was born!

When I was diagnosed with a Learning Disability in the third grade, I'm sure my parents were wondering what else was going to go wrong with me. Between trying to put food on the table and keeping up with three active boys, I'm sure my parents had their hands full and the last thing they needed or wanted was a "special needs" child. No doubt they were discouraged, frustrated and also heart broken that this was something that we had to deal with in the midst of life's craziness.

Looking back, I know that my parents did the best they could for me. My mom in particular encouraged me and took an interest in my schooling, but both her and dad knew very little, if anything about LD and absolutely nothing about ADD. In 1981, when I was put into the Special Ed classroom, ADD had been known as ADD for just one year, renamed as it was from the completely confusing "Hyperkinetic Disorder of Childhood."

I really wish that my parents had been better informed - it could have made my school days much less frustrating and painful. Unfortunately, back when I was a kid, not even the scientists, doctors or teachers knew as much about Learning Disorders as they do today, so I guess my parents can be let off with a light wrist slap. If your child has ADD today, I'm afraid you might not be able to get off the hook so easily. Resources are plentiful and accessible, so you MUST get actively involved in your child's quest to manage their ADD. Here are ten ways that you can do that:

1. Read everything you can get your hands on about ADD. Educate yourself first and foremost. Know what options, rights and opportunities your child has open to her. Also, get out and meet and network with parents of other ADD children. It can be a wonderful and uplifting experience to be around people who know what you're going through and other parents can be a great source of ideas and information to help you help your child.

2. Make yourself available to share with your child what you know about ADD. (You need to be sensitive in your approach based on your child's age and personality. For example, a younger child may need for you to take the initiative to sit down and have "a talk", whereas a teenager may need more "space" and you should wait for them to come to you

to have the conversation.) Don't sugar coat or omit important information, but also, don't scare them or over-dramatize. The idea is to give your child a sense of control by providing relevant information that will help demystify their diagnosis and prevent their over-active imaginations from going wild.

3. Examine your own attitude towards ADD and how you now view your child. Are you disappointed? Scared? Angry? Take the time to be aware of any negative feelings and to figure out why you feel the way you do. I know this sounds all touchy feely, but the truth is unless you understand what's going through your own mind, you won't be able to offer your child the level of support and encouragement that he needs in order to successfully bring his ADD under control. Set aside any expectations and ambitions you may have had for your son or daughter and encourage them to pursue those interests where they show the greatest aptitude and giftedness...even if they are non-traditional or unorthodox.

4. Pay particular attention to your child's self-esteem and work hard to boost it at every turn. Praise her when she succeeds at even the smallest thing. Remember that ADDers love praise and thrive on recognition. It may be very hard to find praise-worthy things about her, but you must try. This is crucial!

5. Involve your child in any decision-making you can. Anything from what brand cookies to buy at the supermarket to the best place in the house for him

to do homework. (Kids usually feel like they have no say in anything anyway, as they struggle for their independence.) A diagnosis of any perceived disability will only convince him further that his life is completely out of his control. This may lead to an attitude of apathy, causing your offspring to use the word "whatever", far more frequently than you can handle. Offering opportunities to make decisions (and then live with the consequences of those decisions), should help him begin to gain a sense of ownership and control over his life.

6. If the "techniques" and "strategies" you have been using to help your child are not working, don't be afraid to try something different! It's easy to fall into the trap of thinking that because your child is the one with the challenge that she should be the one to make changes in her behavior, but this is counter productive thinking. It's up to the adults to be creative and think outside the box. Sometimes only after we make changes in our attitudes and behaviors can we open the door for our child to respond in a positive way.

7. Create a fun reward system. Along with generous praise, kids with ADD are motivated and respond very well to tangible displays of appreciation.

8. The parent with the best organizational abilities should partner up with their child to help them set realistic goals in any and all areas of their life. Break down big tasks into small chunks and celebrate the completion of every stage of the project. Consistency in doing this will give your child an opportunity to

experience and savor the feeling of "success" and accomplishment. That is a reward in itself and will serve to motivate him to continue setting goals.

9. Watch what you say to your child and how you say it. Become aware of your tone and facial expressions when speaking with her. ADDers are notoriously sensitive and perceptive - they will pick up on the smallest nuances of negativity or sarcasm and spend hours obsessing about the conversation. Never put down or tease your child - they will be hurt deeply and it will take one hundred kind words to undo one negative one. Build 'em up, don't break 'em down!

10. It is entirely possible that you yourself have ADD - it runs in families (both my mom and younger brother have it). If so, take it easy on yourself. Take the time out to reward yourself for being the best parent you can be. Take a break from your parental responsibilities, even if just for the afternoon, and treat yourself to some "me" time. Parents need to be praised and rewarded as well for all our hard work!

In the words of Richard D. Lavoie, a highly regarded authority on learning disabilities: "Remember: Your child's self-esteem will be determined by the conditional acceptance that he receives from others - and the unconditional acceptance that he receives from you." Be sure to make your child feel truly special. Learn to see past a cluster of "symptoms" to their uniqueness and giftedness, then teach them to fully embrace a life that is "simply special."

About the author...

When he was in the third grade, Ben was diagnosed with a Learning Disability associated with his reading and writing skills. Had the definition of ADHD existed back then, he would have been diagnosed with that as well. Like most LD/ADHD challenged students, Ben spent the greater majority of his school career struggling to keep up, wondering what was wrong with him, having little guidance and support, going through highs and lows and dealing with self-esteem issues.

Fortunately, Ben didn't allow his challenges to get in the way of becoming a success story. Through trial and error, significant life events, and special people, Ben has learned how to tap into the talents and positive traits that come along with having a Learning Disability & ADHD.

A full-time speaker and entertainer since 1994, Ben has traveled all over the world to share his inspiring, dynamic and creative presentations with people of all ages and backgrounds.

Finally, as much as Ben loves being a speaker and performing artist, he loves being a husband and father more. Married for over eleven years, he, his wife and two daughters live in a great little city called Indianapolis.

Recommended reading:

The following are books that I have read and found to be very helpful:

Anything about ADHD by **Thom Hartmann**, but especially,
ADD Success Stories
ADHD Secrets of Success

Anything by **Edward M. Hallowell & John J. Ratey**, but especially,
Answers to Distraction - Read this first. It's set up in an easy to read Question & Answer format.
Driven to Distraction
Delivered from Distraction

You Mean I'm Not Lazy, Stupid or Crazy?! By **Kate Kelly & Peggy Ramundo**

For parents: The Gift of ADHD by **Lara Honos-Webb**

For teachers: Marching to a Different Drum: Successful Learning for All Kids by **Arthur P. Attwell**

For teens and by teens: A Bird's-Eye View of Life with ADD and ADHD: Advice From Young Survivors by **Chris Zeigler Dendy & Alex Zeigler**

Overall great book for teens to read. Covers everything from relationships to goal setting to eating right: The 7 Habits of Highly Effective Teens by **Sean Covey**

To order copies of this book,
and other ADHD related items,
please visit our online store at

www.chalkguy.com.

Keep your eyes open for
additional titles in the
Simply Special series of books.